1 0 STEPS TO

Successful Coaching

Sophie Oberstein

PRESS

Alexandria, Virginia

ASTD Press is an internationally renowned source of insightful and practical information on workplace learning and performance topics, including training basics, evaluation and return-on-investment (ROI), instructional systems development (ISD), e-learning, leadership, and career development.

Ordering information: Books published by ASTD Press can be purchased by visiting our website at store.astd.org or by calling 800.628.2783 or 703.683.8100.

Library of Congress Control Number: 2009920424

ISBN-10: 1-56286-544-7
ISBN-13: 987-1-56286-544-3

ASTD Press Editorial Staff
Director: Dean Smith
Manager, Acquisitions & Author Relations: Mark Morrow
Editorial Manager: Jacqueline Edlund-Braun
Senior Associate Editor: Tora Estep
Editorial Assistant: Gina Del Priore
Copyeditor: Christine Cotting
Indexer: April Davis
Proofreader: Kris Patenaude
Interior Design: UpperCase Publication Services, Ltd.
Production: UpperCase Publication Services, Ltd.
Cover Design: Ana Ilieva Foreman

Printed by Victor Graphics, Inc., Baltimore, Maryland, www.victorgraphics.com

C O N T E N T S

Let's face it, most people spend their days in chaotic, fast-paced, time- and resource-strained organizations. Finding time for just one more project, assignment, or even learning opportunity—no matter how career enhancing or useful—is difficult to imagine. The *10 Steps* series is designed for today's busy professional who needs advice and guidance on a wide array of topics ranging from project management to people management, from business planning strategy to decision making and time management, from return-on-investment to conducting organizational surveys and questionnaires. Each book in this ASTD series promises to take its readers on a journey to basic understanding, with practical application the ultimate destination. This is truly a just-tell-me-what-to-do-now series. You will find action-driven language teamed with examples, worksheets, case studies, and tools to help you quickly implement the right steps and chart a path to your own success. The *10 Steps* series will appeal to a broad business audience from middle managers to upper-level management. Workplace learning and human resource professionals along with other professionals seeking to improve their value proposition in their organizations will find these books a great resource.

PREFACE

I believe that really effective supervisors always have been terrific coaches. I believe there are coaches among us, disguised as our colleagues, friends, and family members. These are the people we know we can count on to listen to us, encourage us, challenge us, and help us achieve our biggest dreams.

Many of them make the conscious choice to act as that sounding board and champion; others don't even realize they're doing anything out of the ordinary and are surprised when their colleagues consider them to be great coaches.

I am one of those people who chose to develop coaching skills. To be honest, I wasn't naturally approachable in the workplace and didn't believe my personality was "bubbly" enough to be effective as a coach. But after working as a corporate trainer for almost 20 years, I began to find that pulling people away from their jobs to attend classroom training wasn't working anymore. To appeal to a diverse audience, the content of these workshops was too watered down. Many of the situations discussed didn't apply to the people in the room—each with his or her own level of knowledge and experience about the topic. So, in my last job, as employee development manager for the city of Redwood City, California, I changed our development strategy and brought customized, relevant, one-on-one interventions to the individuals in the workplace. In essence, I invented my own type of coaching, and it had a powerful, positive impact not only on the recipients but also on me. I found myself happier and more effective at producing growth and development. I decided to learn more.

10 Steps to Successful Coaching summarizes what I've learned on my coaching journey, and it offers a meaningful process for embracing your existing coaching skills and interjecting more of them into your current work style and environment. Coaching uses the strengths you already have as a leader, colleague, or employee to bring out the strengths of others. As such, it's not about scrapping who you are to become someone else. It's just about connecting with others in a new way. It's about adding new exercises, processes, and questions to the work you do to produce results that are more rewarding and exciting.

My goal for the book is to help you become happier in your role as manager, employee, friend, partner, or parent by becoming more coach-like in your daily interactions.

I've experienced this process as both client and coach, and I've seen the transformations it can produce, so I'm excited for you in what you're about to undertake.

Acknowledgments

I am grateful to the following people for introducing me to the terrific coaches in their lives: Sheryl Gittings, Joyce Irby, Sarah Larson, and Hassan Ramay. And to these terrific coaches who shared some of their greatness with me: Matt Ahrens, Lois Albrecht, Christine Bennett, Robert Cornish, Maria Danly, Tathagata Dasgupta, Meade Dickerson, Ben Dooley, Chris Emery, Laura Goodrich, Maggie Graham, Patricia Katz, Steve Mitten, Caryn Siegel, Marla Skibbins, Barry Weiss, and Susan Wynne. I'd be remiss if I didn't also thank CTI and my wonderful course leaders there for the amazing preparation you gave me.

A huge thank-you to Deanne Bryce, my initial reviewer; to Tara Marcus for putting Deanne and me back in touch; and to Paul Hilt, for getting me reconnected to my audience. Thanks also to Brian Gardner for my author photo.

Finally, I am indebted to all of my current and former clients for letting me learn and grow with you. I'm honored to have been your coach. Thanks, too, for giving me permission to include some of your stories here. My indebtedness extends to my friends and family, who have supported me wholeheartedly in my own transition first as a coaching client and then as a coach. Special thanks to Nina and Ted Liebman, who laid the foundation by raising me in the greatest of rich and supportive environments, and to Sandy and Barry Oberstein, who did the same for my terrific husband. As is everything, Jeff, Lily, and Evan, this is for you.

Sophie Oberstein
April 2009

INTRODUCTION

◆ *Joan managed four employees who'd lost their edge. Sure, they still got their work done and met all performance targets, but they didn't seem to be thinking as creatively as they once had. They didn't seem to be having any fun and no longer seemed passionate about their work.*

◆ *It had always been assumed that Larry would move into his boss's position when the boss retired. But one week after the retirement was announced, Larry made his own announcement: He was leaving to take another job. In an exit interview, he explained that he didn't see a fit for himself with his boss's job. He didn't want a "desk job" and didn't want to keep the hours his boss had kept.*

◆ *Amy was an exceptional manager. Her staff adored her. She'd made huge strides for her department and always got glowing reviews. Lately, however, co-workers could sense that she was stressed. She had less time for people, often interrupted them, and was always rushed and abrupt. When asked, she said that she felt overwhelmed. When she was at work, she felt like she was cheating her employer by not being able to give her all; and when she was at home, she felt the same way about cheating her family.*

For a long time, these types of workplace issues were commonplace, but they weren't regarded as anything managers really should, or could, address. Today, however, individuals in organizations are more willing to take on these types of issues. In fact, they are being asked to do so. One of the ways that managers have been tackling them is by adding coaching skills to their repertoires.

As table I.1 indicates, coaching has evolved in the workplace over the past decade. Once seen as a punishment for being "rough around the edges," coaching is now a perk for those being groomed for positions of greater responsibility. Coaching skills are becoming critical management competencies as organizations prepare a new generation of leaders, using fewer financial, human, and training resources. An explosion in the coaching market in recent years highlights the fact that the work environment continues to be complex, fast-paced, and pressured, and that employees at all levels can derive value from personalized, skilled help delivered in a structured, safe, one-on-one situation. Additionally, the number of people turning to life coaches outside of work demonstrates a new level of acceptance for seeking help to get more out of life.

Coaching isn't just about patting people on the back or providing enthusiastic encouragement. It's a powerful management tool to help employees realize their career aspirations. When managers and supervisors master the art of coaching, their relationships with their direct reports are strengthened—and that often translates to increased company loyalty and enhanced motivation among those reports.

Who Should Read This Book?

This book is an entry point for managers who want to initiate a formal coaching process with their employees, and for anyone who wants to infuse his or her day-to-day interactions in the workplace with a powerful new skill—development through coaching. Employees at all levels, with varying degrees of experience, can benefit from the activities and exercises included here. The book also is for readers who understand that applying these skills will help them in their broader lives. Each of the 10 steps ends with ideas for using its concepts as part of a coaching process or informally in the daily activities of managing others.

This is a primer, so those who have been through a coaching program in the past may find it a good review and may pick up some new exercises or tools. But, chiefly, it is for people who've

TABLE I.1

Coaching Trends

Coaching Then (a Decade or So Ago)	Coaching Now
Considered a punishment for "bad" managers and those who were "rough around the edges"	Considered a perk for employeess with potential; is a retention tool for high-performing managers
Provided by internal HR professionals and trainers or by hired external coaches	Essential leadership attribute
Stand-alone activity	Part of organizational initiatives, such as succession planning; is used in concert with mentoring and organizational networking
Directive, focused on specific skills or goals	Either directive or nondirective, emphasizing the learning process and ongoing growth and development
Less known and understood; membership in the International Coach Federation (ICF) was just under 4,000 in 1999	Growing and more accepted profession; ICF membership increased to more than 14,000 in 2008

only just recognized—or been intrigued by—the power of coaching. Maybe you've witnessed a great coach in action; maybe you realize your direct reports aren't working to their full potential, or that you aren't working to your potential as a leader. Maybe you simply want more out of your experience at work—the chance to connect with others at a deeper level and to promote learning and growth on the job.

This book won't turn you into a coach, but it will make you more coach-like. Let me try an imperfect metaphor to show you the difference. Sometimes, when I'm feeling sick, I have to go to a trained and licensed medical doctor. She can deal with my more serious health concerns and she knows the right doses of medication for me to take. At other times when I'm not feeling 100 percent, I just need someone to make me a bowl of chicken soup or to send me to bed. Some of the best medical advice I've gotten has been from nurses taking my temperature before the doctor comes into the room or from a fellow patient in the waiting room.

In the same way, sometimes an employee needs to work with a trained and experienced coach. His issues might be more all encompassing than his manager feels prepared to handle, he might need someone who's fully trained to work with a broad spectrum of emotional responses, or he might just need the confidentiality an outside party can provide. At other times, all an employee needs to feel more balanced and in control is you—someone who can be coach-like—pulling out tools and asking questions that make him feel better.

There certainly are some purists out there who would say that if it isn't a certified coach using a certain coaching model, it isn't coaching. I ask, Why does that matter? If the employee feels and performs better as a result of the attention of someone acting like a coach, it doesn't matter what you call it. You can even call it coaching.

A Note About Naming

While we're on the subject of what to call things, I have to admit I had some trouble figuring out what to call the people you'll be coaching. Some of you will do this informally with your colleagues, direct reports, or friends. Others will do it in a more structured manner either with people you know and work with or with strangers. So I couldn't describe them all as co-workers or direct reports. I call the people I coach "clients," but that implies some sort of formal business relationship that some of you may not have. That term is also a little more clinical than I like. So I went with the made-up word "coachee" (much to my spell-check's dismay!). If "coachee" doesn't describe the person sitting in front of you, please feel free to substitute whatever word works for you and insert that word wherever I refer to the coachee in these pages.

Sequence of the Steps

In coaching, I try to hold what I call a "soft focus." That is, I have a focus I need to keep my client aware of—one that the two of us create together—but I also need to be free to let go of that agenda to work with what my client is presenting to me at the moment. I can't be rigid about what we're doing together. I have to maintain the focus but be free to move from it.

This need for flexibility could make it difficult to put the work of a coach into a series of sequenced steps, but the more I look at the prevailing coaching models, the more I see that there is some order to coaching. Therefore, I recommend you address these 10 steps with a soft focus, following the logical and proven methods but being willing to bend when the situation requires. You'll want to keep the step sequence in mind as an ideal way to do things—and you'll want to remember that there will be times you won't follow this sequence. You may complete a step and find you have to go back to it. For instance, you may have agreed on the logistics of your coaching relationship in Step 3 but find you have to revisit them later when you're on Step 7. During your first conversation, your coachee may jump ahead to Step 8: Realign When Things Go Bad. Once realigned, you can resume Step 1. You may find that one step takes only a few minutes and another takes a few months. All of these variations are workable when you have a soft focus—an awareness of where you want to be, but one to which you're not wedded.

Another way to use this book is to put it right in to practice. Read Steps 1 and 2, and then pick a coachee. Do the rest of the steps one-by-one with your coachee. Explain to her or him that you're learning as you go so that at each step you'll be practicing different skills and adding more exercises during your interactions.

Remember, too, that you can use the tools and ideas in each step even if you aren't doing a formal, step-by-step process. Using what's offered here in any of your day-to-day interactions as a manager will produce better results from your employees and deepen your relationships with them.

An Overview of the 10 Steps

◆ **Step 1: Prepare Yourself for the Coaching Role**—Before you can coach others, you have to spend some time thinking about what coaching means to you, what your coaching goals are, and what characteristics you need to embody to achieve those goals.

◆ **Step 2: Remove Personal Obstacles**—Aside from the practical considerations of being a coach to your employees addressed in Step 1, there is some deeper preparation that it would benefit you to undertake. Being a coach demands focus and mental energy. If you really want to coach, you have to be willing to look inward. You have to know yourself, what you're capable of, and what you want to avoid. You have to be able to be present with whatever your coachee brings your way. You may need to unload some emotional baggage—including a lack of confidence in your ability to coach—before you can be effective. Only after you've considered these issues yourself will you be able to address them with your coachees.

◆ **Step 3: Create Your Coaching Relationship(s)**—It's one thing to ready yourself for coaching; it's another thing completely to articulate what you want to do for others and to find the right people to coach. When you put yourself out there as a coach, you are displaying vulnerability, strength, and marketing savvy all at once. This is also the step during which you'll discuss how you and your coachee will work together—a very important foundation for the coaching process.

◆ **Step 4: Find Out About Your Coachee**—A coaching relationship can be a powerful engine for growth and change, but only if there is a deep sense of trust between coach and coachee and if the coachee truly feels known by the coach. Creating this in-depth relationship is the foundation of coaching and will set you and your coachee on the path to success. You'll use this knowledge of your coachee and how he or she "works" over and over again in the later steps.

◆ **Step 5: Agree on What You Want to Accomplish**—Even some of the most eager coachees sometimes enter a coaching relationship unsure about their focus issues and goals. They may be unaware of some of the areas in which they need coaching, although their bosses, colleagues, or friends can see them clearly. Coaching goals need to focus not only on what coachees want to accomplish, but also on who they want to become as they accomplish these things. As such, agreeing on what the two of you want to accomplish through your work together is more than just standard goal setting. To ensure that coaching actually is closing the gap between where the coachee is and where he or she wants to be, accountability that comes from establishing these expectations has to be built into the relationship.

◆ **Step 6: Use the Power of Possibility**—Coaching comes from an expansive rather than a limiting place. Coaches need to help their coachees think more broadly about themselves and what they're capable of accomplishing. Responding to powerful questions posed by their coaches, coachees come to recognize their own greatness and the possibilities that are available to them.

◆ **Step 7: Partner to Enhance Growth Between Sessions**— A goal of coaching is to help your coachee become self-sufficient. You can jump-start this process with assignments for coachees to complete between coaching sessions. Assignments serve to help the coachee notice what is happening for her or him, try out new approaches, or take action toward achieving specific goals. The way these assignments are created and given is quite different from the way you remember getting homework!

◆ **Step 8: Realign When Things Go Bad**—Coaching relationships can unleash more emotion than your standard manager–employee conversation; so, by their very nature, they have the potential to hit potholes. This step will help you recognize the signs that coaching is derailed and then help you learn how to realign the relationship and troubleshoot a variety of problems that can crop up in the coaching process.

- **Step 9: Maintain Positive Changes**—The beginning of a coaching relationship can be exciting and invigorating for both parties. There comes a point, however, when the initial energy is wearing off; when the coachee, who's made significant changes early on in the process, starts to revert to the way she or he used to be or used to do things. Knowing how to coach at this step helps keep your time together from growing stale and helps your coachee continue to move forward.

- **Step 10: Complete the Coaching Cycle**—Many coaching relationships continue long after they've ceased being beneficial. Knowing when and how to end a coaching relationship ensures that the progress you and your coachee have made together is integrated into how the coachee lives and works going forward. Likewise, from each coaching relationship you complete you learn much that will help you continue to be engaged and excited about yourself and your coaching. Bringing an appropriate end to the coaching relationship will help both parties confirm achievements made and lessons learned.

After reading and working through these 10 steps once, review them periodically. They'll inspire you with new questions to ask and new tools to use in your coaching.

Being a coach to the employees you manage can be a very powerful experience. You have the opportunity to inspire those around you to achieve great things for themselves—at work and outside of work—and to experience greater happiness. And, in the process, you'll become more self-aware and effective. So, go forth and coach!

Prepare Yourself for the Coaching Role

OVERVIEW

What is coaching?

What isn't coaching?

What makes a great coach?

Why coach?

In writing this book, I contacted many people whose job descriptions didn't include anything about coaching, but whose colleagues identified them as terrific coaches. Why did they think that these individuals were coach-like?

◆ "He hired us, groomed us, and then pushed us to get promoted and take on positions and roles that were higher than his in the corporate world."—Hassan Ramsey, speaking about Dr. Tathagata Dasgupta, University of California–Irvine

◆ "He mentored and was there for his people."—Joyce Irby, describing Barry Weiss, director of City of San Carlos Parks and Recreation

◆ "He is always the person who finds the potential in others, and in ideas. He finds the reasons to say 'yes' rather than 'no.'"—Sarah Larson, speaking about Chris Emery, director of marketing at Insight Imaging

Though none of the people described above is trained or working as a coach, those who report to them or work alongside them regard them highly for their coaching abilities. The individuals don't see themselves as coaches at all; rather they believe they are simply good leaders. None of them was recognized as a coach for the same reason, and none of them coaches employees in the same way.

What does all this tell us? Quite a bit. First, we learn that there simply is no right way to coach—and we wouldn't want there to be. A one-size-fits-all approach to coaching couldn't be effective for the diverse interests and experiences of individuals in the workplace. That means that you are the very best coach for some particular person and a less-than-ideal coach for someone else. It means that if you coach several people, you might have to do it differently for each one of them. Second, it tells us that you don't need to be trained as a coach to be effective as one. More broadly, it says that anyone can be like a coach to others and that no matter what you do in that role, it will be appreciated.

What Is Coaching?

Asking this question is like asking, What is leadership? The answer depends on whom you ask and where you look. Definitions abound. There's a glut of information available that becomes repetitive at best and often is contradictory. As is true in defining leadership, the important thing in defining coaching is to find which voices in the field you agree with and trust. Find a definition that works for you and stick with it. You'll never get everyone out there to agree, so you just need to find the definition that resonates with you.

Here's the definition I use: Coaching is a meaningful, accountable relationship created by having routine one-on-one conversations about the coachee's full experience and the power of possibility.

Every word in that definition is important. Let's break it down:

◆ **Meaningful**—Coaching is not a superficial conversation. It's not your weekly project check-in or planning meeting (although, if you have no other time, these are good places to sneak in a little coaching). Coaching is an opportunity to step outside the day-to-day pressures of work to focus on deeper issues, such as what makes the employee fulfilled and productive at work.

- **Accountable**—Without accountability, coaching conversations are simply that—conversations that don't lead to any lasting change or to growth and development. Coaching includes check-ins on assignments and measurements of progress toward goals.
- **Relationship**—A relationship needs more than one person to make it work. Coaching is a two-way model built on trust and mutuality.
- **Routine**—Coach and coachee should get together with some regularity—and this doesn't mean at annual performance review meetings! You and your coachee will decide what frequency makes sense, depending on your schedules and on the coachee's goals. Regular meetings enhance trust, accountability, and progress.
- **One-on-one**—Just by taking the time to be alone with your employee, you show her you value her and are invested in her growth and development. Deeper, more intimate relationships are formed when two people work together as coach and coachee.
- **Full experience**—When you come into the office, you don't check your outside life at the door. Whatever is going on for you at home comes to work with you, and vice versa. Wherever you are, you're a whole person living a full experience. When a coach shies away from allowing the coachee to share her full experience, the coach is discounting that person's values, dreams, and motivations. Therefore, there are practically no limits on what can be included in a coaching conversation.
- **Power of possibility**—Coaches have to encourage their coachees. When a coachee doesn't believe in herself, or when no one else believes in her, the coach has to help illuminate the power of possibility for the coachee—help her understand what choices actually are available and let her make conscious choices. Uncovering possibilities helps people get out of situations in which they're stuck or in

conflict. This component of coaching often requires coaches to show coachees the greatness within them that makes their success possible.

That's my definition. If it doesn't resonate with you, try some of the following ways to arrive at your own definition:

- Think about someone who's been a good coach to you. This need not be someone who was acting officially as your coach. It need not have been in the workplace; maybe it was a teacher, a sports coach, or someone from well in your past. Make a list of this person's best qualities. What did she or he do that was coach-like? Pose the same questions to people around you to get their input. Use the characteristics and examples on your list to craft your own definition of coaching. So, if you remember that your high school guidance counselor was a great coach to you because she displayed good listening skills and she created a plan for you that was completely individualized, you might come up with a definition something like this: "A coach is a person who listens intently to guide you on a personal journey."

- Enter the keywords *coach* and *definition* in Google or another search engine and see what comes up. Look for themes among the definitions and words or phrases to which you relate. Use all of these pieces to craft a definition that works for you. Here are a few of the definitions for *coach* that I found in a recent search:
  - a railroad passenger car or motor bus
  - a person who trains or directs athletes or athletic teams
  - someone who supports, explains, demonstrates, instructs, and directs others via encouragement and questions; may include lifestyle advice, such as nutrition, exercise, behavior, and more
  - an ongoing professional relationship that helps people produce extraordinary results in their lives, careers, businesses, or organizations
  - a task in which the coach supports the client in professional matters to develop the client's own resources and solution-finding capabilities.

From those definitions, you might come up with something like this: "Coaching is moving people from one place to another in support of ongoing training or a specifically desired result."

What Isn't Coaching?

Although I allow for much latitude in defining what coaching is, I am pretty passionate about declaring what coaching is not. I'd like to debunk a few common myths about coaching. You've probably heard them before—you may even ascribe to some of them.

◆ **Myth #1: Coaching is giving advice.** Actually, coaching involves asking the questions that the coachee wouldn't think to ask herself so that she can access her own answers. It's intended to help people whose perspectives are so ingrained that they can't see their blindspots come to a new awareness of themselves. A coach needs to get rid of his own inclinations to give advice or to solve problems, even when the coachee is asking what she should do. Why is that? Why don't coaches give advice? First, providing advice builds dependency when you really want your coachees to solve their own problems and make their own decisions. Second, the advice you give may not be the advice that the coachee needs or that works for her at that moment. It may be something she's already tried that hasn't produced the results she wanted, or it might not inspire her to action. Third, there is no shortage of advice in people's lives. What's missing is a technique to process that advice and to figure out what advice makes the most sense to the coachee. That's where a coach comes in. Finally, coaches should not be wedded to any one solution or technique; and when the coach is the source of advice, he often expects the coachee to take it. Give advice and you're an adviser; help the coachee discover her own best advice and you're a coach.

◆ **Myth #2: The value of a coach is his knowledge and experience in the coachee's area of interest or endeavor.**

In fact, you can get great coaching from someone whose experience is completely unrelated to your current circumstances, or from someone who is your junior in chronological age or working years. A coach's value lies in helping the coachee access her own knowledge and experience and bring them to bear on current circumstances and future goals. The spotlight is on the greatness in the coachee, not on the greatness or expertise of the coach. That's what sets a coach apart from a mentor, whose value *is* based on his knowledge and experience and how he can impart them to his protégé.

◆ **Myth #3: Coaching is just like therapy.** If you listen to an individual coaching session, it may sound like therapy. Deep issues are being discussed and emotions are welcome. But there are two primary differences between coaching and therapy. The first difference relates to the severity of the presenting circumstances in the coachee's life. The second difference is the absence of any analysis of how a coachee came to be in her current circumstances. Coaches won't ask, What happened in your past to bring you to this situation? Instead, they'll take it at face value that this is where the coachee is. It's rather like saying you're here and you want to get over there, so let's get moving! Coaching has a present and future focus, and it doesn't delve into the past as therapy might.

> **POINTER**
>
> The greatest good you can do for another is not just to share your riches, but to reveal to him his own. – *Benjamin Disraeli, statesman and writer*

◆ **Myth #4: The coach drives the coaching process.** I once was looking for individuals to become coaches in an organization and was met with very limited response. As I tried to understand why, I was told that in the company's previous coaching program, the people who'd volunteered as coaches had gotten burned out. They'd worked really hard on their coachees' behalf—some had been doing such things as writing résumés or presentations for their coachees. It took me a long time to break through this mindset and help the potential coaches in my program understand that the actual driver of the coaching process is the coachee. She sets the agenda for meetings, she works in concert with the coach to craft the assignments she will complete, and she takes action in her situation. It's also true that what she puts into coaching is in direct proportion to what she gets out of it. When the coach calls the meeting, determines the agenda, and assigns the homework, the coach is acting as the employee's boss. Workplace coaching is especially challenging in this regard. How do you go from being someone's boss in some situations to being her coach in another? (This will be addressed in Step 3.) Coaching is a delicate two-way relationship, and the coach does have an important role to play in keeping to the focus the coachee has set, providing feedback on how the process of coaching is going, and checking in for accountability. It's just that coaching is for the coachee, so she gets to create it and to be responsible for it.

What Makes a Great Coach?

Maybe you are a natural-born coach, or maybe there are some skills for you to learn. Worksheet 1.1 will help you determine how you measure up against several competencies important for coaches. Please note that the list of competencies is not necessarily comprehensive. As much as I'd like to, I can't provide an exhaustive list of qualities or characteristics that a coach needs to have. However, the list in worksheet 1.1 takes into account the competencies put forth by the International Coach Federation (the authoritative source for all things related to coaching) and several other existing programs and models, as well as my own experience.

POINTER

It's never too late to be who you might have been. – George Eliot, author

WORKSHEET 1.1

My Coaching Competencies

Instructions: For each competency listed in the first column (and described in column 2), consider how your employees or co-workers would rate you— poor, fair, good, or excellent. Circle the appropriate term in the third column. Feel free to also ask a few people to complete the survey for you. Tell them you'll appreciate their honest responses because it's part of your development as a coach.

Competency	Description	How am I doing in this area?
Self-management	Do you know your own strengths and weaknesses? Can you maintain focus on your coachee, rather than on what is going on for you?	Poor Fair Good Excellent
Listening actively	Do you practice the skill of active listening by focusing on the speaker and reflecting the essence of what she's said? Do people come to you because you are a good listener? Do you "listen" to nonverbal communication?	Poor Fair Good Excellent
Being curious	Do you want to know all that you can about people? Do you ask questions to uncover what the people you are talking to are experiencing? Do you have a natural curiosity?	Poor Fair Good Excellent
Asking powerful questions	Can you stop people in their tracks with a question that gets them thinking? Do you know the benefits of questioning rather than providing answers?	Poor Fair Good Excellent
Refraining from giving advice	Can you hold your advice back to let the coachee discover her own best advice? Do you help employees find their own solutions? Can you refrain from butting in when the coachee's own answers aren't what you had in mind for her?	Poor Fair Good Excellent
Keeping confidentiality	Do you treat confidentiality as essential? Do you refrain from sharing with others the "stuff" that happens at work? Do you keep private what you hear in private? Do you get permission before sharing someone else's experience? Do you leave out names and identifying information when sharing stories?	Poor Fair Good Excellent

Worksheet 1.1, continued

Competency	Description	How am I doing in this area?
Being present	Can you put the rest of the day's urgencies out of your mind to be there for your coachee? Can you shut off the phone, email, and all other distractions? Can you be in the moment?	Poor Fair Good Excellent
Consistently making time	Do you regularly meet with employees? Do you keep meetings with them as sacred as you do those with clients or customers? Do you get back to people within 24 hours of their initial contact?	Poor Fair Good Excellent
Giving constructive feedback	Do you have a healthy attitude toward feedback as a development tool, and do you offer feedback that is specific and helpful? Do you provide regular feedback about your employees' job performance? Do you hold postmortems at the end of projects or at other significant milestones?	Poor Fair Good Excellent
Partnering to create assignments that move your coachee to action	How are you at brainstorming? Can you think creatively about what your coachee might do to move toward her goal? How well do you solicit the input of others when solving problems? Are you a motivator?	Poor Fair Good Excellent
Planning and goal setting	How are you at creating action plans? Do you work with a timeline? Can you create goals that are specific, measurable, realistic, and time-bound?	Poor Fair Good Excellent
Establishing accountability	Do you set and communicate standards of excellence and expectations? Do you follow up with those to whom you've delegated? Do you create accountability?	Poor Fair Good Excellent
Creating a coaching relationship through expectations and agreements	Are you explicit about the roles you play with your employees? Do you establish mutually acceptable agreements about how you will work with someone? Do you clarify how each of you best communicates at the start of a work relationship or project?	Poor Fair Good Excellent

continued on next page

STEP 1

Competency	Description	How am I doing in this area?
Being flexible	Are you willing and able to switch gears as needed? Can you think on your feet and make new decisions as new information becomes available? Do you provide freedom for your employees to do their jobs?	Poor Fair Good Excellent
Establishing trust and intimacy	Do people come to you with their problems? Do you have friends in the workplace? Do people trust you to do what you say you will do? Will you not shy away from emotional people and reactions?	Poor Fair Good Excellent
Respecting and appreciating the coachee	Do you view your employees as partners and see them as critical to your own success? Would you be happy for them if their accomplishments were greater than your own? Do you see their greatness and believe in them? Do you know the strengths of each of your employees and capitalize on those strengths? Do you look for the good in your colleagues and direct reports?	Poor Fair Good Excellent
Being open to the coachee's whole experience	Do you protect your employees from undue stress? Do you creatively encourage work/life balance? Do you see work as just one component of your own or your colleague's life?	Poor Fair Good Excellent
Thinking big for the coachee	Do you push people to do more than they think they are capable of doing? Do you encourage big ideas and dreams? Are you more a yes-sayer than a naysayer?	Poor Fair Good Excellent
Providing recognition	Do you give your employees credit when they deserve it? Do you celebrate successes? Do you balance your constructive feedback with positive reinforcement?	Poor Fair Good Excellent
Reading a situation	Can you read the energy in a room? Are you as aware of what's not being said as of what is being communicated directly? Do you have strong intuition?	Poor Fair Good Excellent

After assessing your current coaching competencies and with the definition of coaching fresh in your mind, it's time to consider some questions as you clarify and commit to your coaching role. The questions in worksheet 1.2 will highlight your existing coaching strengths to increase your level of confidence as you embark on coaching. They also help you identify the skills and characteristics you'll want to bolster to be more effective as a coach to your employees.

WORKSHEET 1.2

My Coaching Development Plan

Instructions: Respond to the questions that follow. Questions 1 and 2 highlight your existing coaching strengths. Feel free to include those competencies rated highest on Worksheet 1.1 here, or other skills you possess that will make you effective as a coach. Questions 3, 4, and 5 focus on how you might want to improve as a coach. Answering them will give you a vision of what you seek to achieve as a coach and a plan for achieving it.

1. What leadership skills do I have that will serve me well as a coach?

2. What other skills/characteristics do I have that will serve me well as a coach?

3. What aspects of coaching will be a stretch for me?

4. In an area that's going to be a stretch for me, what does excellence look like? What will be happening when I am consistently excelling at performing this aspect of coaching?

5. What is something I can do today to move closer to a rating of "excellent" in that area?

Why Coach?

Why should there be coaching in the workplace? Couldn't managers get great results from their folks just by being good role models or setting expectations and making people aware of them? Why should you talk to employees about their full experience?

You picked up this book, so I'm assuming there is something drawing you to coaching. What excites you about being more coach-like in your interactions with your co-workers? This is a good place to pause and think about that question before you move any further. If it's helpful, use the Notes section at the end of this step to record your thoughts.

> **POINTER**
>
> I personally do not think of my own benefits when I coach. The sparkle in a student's eyes, the text message from a client who got a promotion, or the improved deliverable from a subordinate are rewards. But there is a learning process involved—I learn as much as I coach. – *Tathagata Dasgupta, Ph.D., adjunct faculty, operations and decision technologies, Paul Merage School of Business, University of California–Irvine*

Worksheet 1.3 is an exercise to help you determine the benefits *you* will reap from coaching. The worksheet presents a list of many possible—and real—benefits of coaching. It's important to know what drives you to coach your employees so that when the going gets tough, when you just can't imagine how you'll fit coaching into your already busy day, you can refer to the list of motivations and benefits you find most compelling. There are no wrong answers to the exercise. It's simply your personal reminder of why you want to coach.

Now that you know why you personally want to increase your coaching repertoire, you'll find tool 1.1 interesting. It presents some of the benefits that more generally are ascribed to coaching for the organization, the coach, and the person being coached.

Arguments for the power of workplace coaching are increasing in proportion to its increased incidence. This is no surprise,

WORKSHEET 1.3

Why Should I Coach?

Instructions: In this exercise, you'll distribute 200 points among your top motivations for integrating coaching skills into your management competencies. First, select your four top reasons and place a checkmark to the left of each one. Then give each of those four reasons one of the following point values: 100, 50, 25, and 25. Assigning points thoughtfully prioritizes your coaching motivations and reveals what benefits you expect to realize from the endeavor.

Motivation/Benefit	Points
• Incorporating coaching is an opportunity to advance my own career.	
• I can use my strong skills to help others grow.	
• I have a passion for learning.	
• I can give people skills that can help them.	
• I will become a better communicator.	
• I will become a better partner, parent, family member, or friend.	
• Coaching will promote a more productive workplace.	
• I'd like to become a coach on my own some day.	
• It's just the way to be with people.	
• I will become more efficient in my own work practices.	
• I will get better results from my staff.	
• I will be a better leader.	
• I want to help an employee who needs her rough edges refined.	
• If I integrate coaching skills, our team will get along better.	
• Coaching is part of my job description.	
• I want to further my own learning and growth.	
• I want to become more open to feelings—mine and others'.	
• I want to be available to others; everyone needs someone to talk to.	
• I want to improve the world.	
• I want to give to others.	
• Other [add your own motivation/expected benefit]:	

TOOL 1.1

Coaching Benefits

Benefits to the organization	Benefits to managers/coaches	Benefits to employees
• Cost-effective development occurs on the job and is customized for each employee.	• They develop skills and receive tools to coach employees.	• Increased motivation and productivity result from personal attention.
• Responsibility for developing employees is decentralized.	• Using coaching skills enhances all of their working relationships.	• They receive individualized and confidential advice on issues affecting their careers.
• Manager–employee relationships are strengthened.	• Their teams become more cohesive and productive.	• Morale and job satisfaction increase as they experience the fulfillment coming from doing work that honors their values.
• Productivity increases.	• They feel a sense of accomplishment as they reach their own goals; their performance often improves.	
• When employees explore their interests and skills, a good fit between them and their work is ensured.		• Confidence increases.
• High-potential employees are less likely to leave organizations that invest resources to help them meet their needs and interests.		• The discovery that real choices are available to them is empowering.

knowing what we know about the most effective strategies for maximizing learning. Research by the Center for Creative Leadership has shown that these are the best options for growth:

◆ experience-based options (such as job rotations, temporary assignments, or project management)—70 percent effective

◆ feedback- and relationship-based options (including personality-based profiles, mentoring, or buddy systems)—20 percent effective

◆ education-based options (such as workshops, training courses, or degree programs)—10 percent effective.

Coaching is more than just a feedback- and relationship-based option. Because it encourages coachees to experience new ways of doing things and to take on projects and challenges, it derives benefits from experience-based options; because it often results in coachees enrolling in workshops or getting additional education, it also garners the benefit an education-based option provides.

POINTER

Coach Training

This book will make you more coach-like in your day-to-day interactions. Enrolling in a coach training program will turn you into a bona fide coach. This doesn't necessarily mean that you need to earn your income as a full-time coach (although it often leads to that), but that you'd add value to whatever job you hold as a credentialed coach.

Some of the more well-known coach training programs are Coach Inc., Coach U, Coaches Training Institute (CTI), the Institute for Life Coach Training (ILCT), iPEC Coaching, MentorCoach, New Ventures West Integral Coach Training, and Results Coaching Systems. There are hundreds more. ASTD also offers a two-way Coaching Certificate Program that focuses on workplace learning and performance coaching.

If you decide you want to become a credentialed coach, how do you choose which program to attend? First, make sure the program you're considering is accredited by the International Coach Federation (ICF). Most weekend or three- to six-day coaching programs aren't accredited and, like this book, can only give you some good coaching tools and some ideas. Each of the ICF-accredited programs is described in some detail on the ICF website, under the heading "Coach Training," then "For Prospective Students."

Next, look at the programs' materials—primarily their websites or any published texts. Do they speak to you? Do you agree with their general philosophy and approach? Some programs are more academic in nature, some more contextual. Some programs take a business approach to starting your own coaching practice. Many concentrate on a specific type of coaching, like relationship coaching, corporate coaching, or group coaching.

If the program you're considering offers a free teleclass to introduce you to its curriculum (and many do), sign up for it. Speak to graduates with backgrounds similar to yours to see how they're using what they learned. These programs' administrative staff and counselors are trained to help you make this decision.

Finally, of course, you'll have to factor in your logistical needs. Programs vary greatly in their cost, location, schedule, class size, and flexibility.

Coaching is more than just a buzzword in today's complex work world. Executed with care, coaching is an intimate, significant relationship that truly will affect two people deeply and produce measurable results for organizations.

Applying the Learning

◆ How do you define coaching?

◆ How are your coaching skills? Review your ratings on worksheet 1.1. This week, try to implement the item that will propel you toward excellence (identified in worksheet 1.2).

◆ What is drawing you to coaching? Review the point totals you assigned to the coaching motivations and benefits in worksheet 1.3. This will help ensure that you always know why you're taking the time and energy to do this.

NOTES

Remove Personal Obstacles

Here are some of the reactions I get when I tell people I'm a coach: I could never be a coach. I can't even get my own life/work under control; or How can you coach people in areas that you don't know a lot/anything about?

I, of course, have responses to those reactions: Coaching others isn't about my work; it's about theirs. What's happening—or not happening—in my life doesn't have to affect my coaching. If my life were perfectly ordered, I couldn't relate to the challenges and setbacks that my clients face, and sometimes it takes an external perspective to see a situation more clearly; knowing too many of the technical details of a person's situation might bog down the coaching. It actually can be an asset that I don't know much about what a client is facing.

But what if I didn't believe as I do and didn't understand these situations in this way? I really could get caught up in those obstacles, and they could keep me from coaching. Certainly there are other questions that haven't been as easy for me to answer—questions I had about my own ability to coach (remember that in the

Preface I mentioned my fear that I wasn't enthusiastic [OK, bubbly] enough) and questions about some obstacles in my work environment. Some of the obstacles I faced were real and some were just perceived; some were insurmountable and several, when I'd done some deep thinking about them, were not real problems. Other obstacles I face continually because they come up again and again.

Addressing your obstacles to coaching means coming face-to-face with them—not always the most fun thing to do. Who wants to deal with the "dark side" of something that she or he is anxious to do? You're on a roll—you're ready to coach. I know that many of you will want to skip this step, but please don't. This is one of the steps that's going to set apart an effective workplace coach from someone who simply does a good job creating relationships and motivating enhanced performance.

Besides, at some point in your coaching relationships you are going to be asking your coachees to address their own obstacles. To be authentic in doing so, you'll want to know that you've been willing to do it yourself. Your openness to dealing with challenges in your own life often can come across to coachees in implicit or explicit ways.

And here's the other positive outcome of this exploration. When you're more self-aware, your relationships with others are enhanced—both in and outside of work. You come to know yourself and what you're capable of accomplishing, as well as what your shortcomings are and what you'd prefer not to handle in a coaching format.

Here's a formula for removing your obstacles. It sounds simple, but it turns out not to be so easy to execute. First you have to notice the barriers and then consciously decide what you want to do about them.

Stop Being Too Busy to Notice What's Going On

One of the first obstacles to stellar coaching—or stellar anything, for that matter—is the inability to slow down and notice what's actually going on. *Noticing* is the first step in our plan to overcome obstacles.

The inability to slow down and notice is ubiquitous in our work environments. It's present when something about you is holding you back, and although others can see it, you can't. It's there when you're really nervous about doing something but you plunge in anyway and produce results that are less than you'd imagined. It's even present when you're simply so busy rushing from one fire to another that you have no appreciation or understanding of how you're feeling in the moment.

Here are some simple things you can do to slow yourself down and get in touch with how you feel about coaching, how you're doing as a coach, or how you want a particular coaching discussion to go. These techniques are helpful in other circumstances, too—like when you or your coachee needs to slow down and become aware of what's needed in a given circumstance.

- ◆ **Breathe.** Nothing slows us down, centers us, or calms us like a good deep breath. So simple and yet, when was the last time you took a deep breath in your workplace? We simply don't remember to breathe deeply—deep enough to expand our bellies. I learned a wonderful breathing exercise from my clarinet teacher when I was in junior high school and feeling nervous about an upcoming performance. Try this exercise and see how well it calms you: Breathe in through your nose for 2 seconds and out through your mouth for 4; or in for 5 seconds, out for 10—whatever numbers feel right for you. As you inhale, be sure the air goes down to the bottoms of your lungs and expands your belly. Do this type of breathing four or five times a day. It's even helpful when you have trouble falling asleep.

- ◆ **Slow down part of you.** Maria Danly, one of my amazing instructors at CTI, taught me this technique. Put one arm out in front of you in that classic pose of a waiter carrying a towel across his arm. Put the elbow of the other arm in the upward palm of the extended arm. Now swing the top arm from side to side like a metronome at the speed that your thoughts and your heart are racing. Do that a few times and then cut that speed down to half. Keep the metronome going at half speed and then cut it in half again. Do this again until the arm that's measuring the pace of your thoughts has slowed down almost to a standstill.

◆ Close your eyes and do a **head-to-toe inventory** of how your body is feeling. There's no need to do anything about what you notice. Don't judge what you're feeling or try to "correct" it—just become aware of what is going on in your body. Is your forehead relaxed or scrunched up? Are there butterflies in your stomach or is there a knot in your gut? Do you feel heavy or light?

◆ Find some time to **sit quietly.** Just sit still, especially if it's difficult for you. Spend 10 minutes consciously not think-ing, just noticing. What do you see, hear, smell around you? If your mind starts solving problems, analyzing issues, or doing anything other than consciously noticing, go back to merely sitting still. I'm not suggesting meditation here, just sitting and being aware of your surroundings.

Being able to slow down our highly pressured, fast-paced work and social environments will enable you to notice what's happening for you and to be there for others as a coach. In that way, slowing down removes the obstacle of being disconnected from others as you become present in the current moment and with the coachee sitting in front of you.

What to Do When You're the Obstacle to Good Coaching

In coaching, there's a term for those voices inside your head that keep you from excelling or from trying something new: *gremlins*. You probably have some coaching-focused gremlins right now. Are any of these voices in your self-talk right now?

◆ "Who am I to say I'm an expert/a coach?"

◆ "*[Fill in a name here]* is better at coaching than I am."

◆ "I'll make a fool of myself."

- "I can't handle it when they ask questions I can't answer."
- "I'm OK coaching around performance issues, but not personal issues. Those don't belong in the workplace."

You may have more than one of these voices speaking up right now—and maybe a few I haven't included. If a whole chorus of gremlins is going on inside you right now, that's natural.

Before you can coach others, you need to determine how you're going to respond to these gremlins (also referred to as saboteurs or simply as obstacles). Here are some techniques that coaches use to help coachees handle their internal challenges—techniques that will help you as well:

- **Recognize that these internal voices are stating beliefs, not facts,** and that beliefs can be changed if you notice them and decide you want to change them. Maybe you notice that you believe this: I'm OK coaching around performance issues, but not personal issues. Those don't belong in the workplace. If you hold that belief, it will certainly limit your relationship with your coachee. If coaching involves the coachee's full experience, you can't put a lid on it. But maybe that belief serves you in some other way. How does it help you? How does it harm you? With what other belief might you replace it, if you choose to do so?

- **Notice and name your gremlins.** Are they the ones listed above? Are there others? For example, my gremlin might be this: "Jim, my supervisor, is a better coach than I am." I'll call this gremlin "inferiority." Just naming it helps me recognize when it's present so I can decide what I want to do with it. Naming it takes away its power because I'm no longer just blindly responding to it. I'm calling it out. Now when I catch myself thinking, So-and-So is much better than I am, I can just swoop right in and say, "Oh, there's that darn inferiority again!" (And when inferiority about your coaching abilities does come along, remember that your unique background, skills, awareness, and knowledge make you the very best coach for someone who needs just that mix.)

◆ **Decide what's true** about the gremlin's message and be grateful for it. For example, maybe it's true that I'll look like a fool at first. Thank your gremlin for trying to protect you and help you save face. Gremlins are sneaky because they aren't necessarily malicious and they'd always say they have your best interests at heart. But the way they want to protect you is to keep you from changing or from trying anything new. The truth is you might feel like a fool, and the coachee—so involved in his own thoughts at the time—might not even notice. Plus, you can't learn something new without looking like a fool at times. (When learning to ski, the first thing you're taught is how to fall—and get back up.)

◆ **Decide what's untrue** about the gremlin's message. For instance, you may know that you've handled challenging questions in many situations other than coaching, and that you can do the same thing here. Counter the gremlin's message with this: "When I'm in the public eye and challenged, I can pull something out of my hat."

◆ **Know that coaching gremlins often are related to myths.** Debunking those myths debunks the gremlin voices. For instance, the voice that says, "Who am I to say I'm an expert/a coach?" may be related to the myth that the value of a coach is her knowledge and experience. Remember those myths from Step 1? Which ones are you still carrying with you?

◆ **Decide whether you want to honor, and live by, what the gremlins are saying,** or by what is drawing you to try something new—in this case, coaching. In other words, is your gremlin's message more important than whatever is calling you to coach? If you want to overcome this obstacle to your coaching, tell yourself this: I'm ready to take this challenge because I really want to help people be more satisfied/productive at work. That's why it's useful to have those benefits from Step 1 nearby—

to help you recall why you're doing this, sometimes against the wisdom of your inner gremlin's voice.

Controlling your self-talk during coaching is immensely important. This includes knowing your gremlins and how you want to manage them. Then you can listen intently to what your coachee is saying rather than to the voices inside your head that are criticizing you for not doing it "right." Then you'll know where your boundaries are and you can be explicit about your needs when your boundaries are crossed during a coaching situation. Worksheet 2.1

WORKSHEET 2.1

Managing My Coaching Gremlins

Instructions: Answer the questions below to identify your own gremlins and decide how you want to handle them.

My gremlin's name is			
What belief or myth is this gremlin personifying?			
What's true about this gremlin's message?			
What's untrue about this gremlin's message?			
With what belief do I want to replace this gremlin voice, if any?			
What do I want to honor instead of this gremlin, if anything?			

will help you identify and overcome the gremlins that are keeping you from excelling as a coach.

Incidentally, if your coaching gremlins are like those of many other coaches I've met, the countering responses offered in tool 2.1 might help you manage them.

Finding Your Own Coach

One of the best ways to remove your obstacles is to get your own coach. I'm not saying this to drum up business for coaches, nor am I saying that your coach must be a paid, external one. I'm simply suggesting that you may want to make finding a coach part of your own preparation to become a coach. Coaches are really well suited to help you honor what you want to and to put aside the doubts or obstacles that squash your vision or what's important to you.

When my first coaching mentor, Caryn Siegel, and I were creating a coaching curriculum for managers, she told me that the two ways she'd learned most about being a coach were (1) by coaching while being observed and then getting immediate feedback and (2) by observing another coach. We made sure our program included both of those components. You can get these two experiences from a coaching relationship, too. Often you can find a coach who is willing to have you coach her and then give you feedback. You also can observe what your own coach is doing and ask questions about why she did what she did.

The biggest reason I know that I and other coaches get coaches of our own is to walk our talk. How am I going to coach others if I'm not willing to address issues and move toward greatness in my own life? Walking your talk adds credibility and shows that you truly believe in the power of coaching—so much so that you are sticking with it yourself.

As Marla Skibbins, master certified coach and co-founder of My Full Practice, says, "A coach who is coached knows how difficult it can be to move toward the life one envisions, which enables her to be compassionate and understanding with her own clients'

TOOL 2.1

Responses to Some Common Coaching Gremlins

Gremlin Message	Countering Response
I/We don't have time for coaching.	Although it may be time consuming to provide one-on-one coaching for my employees, ultimately the coaching they receive will help them take initiative and do more—and that will save a great deal of time.
This isn't what I get paid to do.	My performance as a manager is measured by how my employees perform. In a sense, I'm getting paid to do whatever it takes to help them succeed.
My employees don't like this management style.	I won't be fooled by some resistance to my acting like a coach. Expecting to be managed in a certain way isn't the same as preferring it. There may be natural resistance at first (especially when employees don't trust that my new coaching style is here to stay), but many of them will embrace the idea if they believe it's an actual long-term possibility.
I'll lose my authority.	It's hard to lose my authority when I'm gaining the respect of my employees. Actually, I'll be shifting the type of authority I have from authority based on my position to authority based on my relationships and who I am as a leader.
People at this level in the organization should be able to figure things out for themselves; coaching shouldn't be necessary at a certain level.	Coaching is necessary at executive levels precisely because so many people hold this belief. Senior managers have no place to share their concerns or perceived inadequacies because they or those around them feel it shouldn't be necessary—hence, the expression "It's lonely at the top." And research has posited that many executives are derailing because they're relying on the competencies that got them to their current positions rather than on new skills they need to perform effectively. Coaching can help instill those needed skills.

continued on next page

Tool 2.1, continued

Gremlin Message	Countering Response
I'm uncomfortable with confrontation.	Nowhere on the list of coaching competencies is conflict resolution listed. That's because coaching isn't confrontational. As a coach I may have to be outspoken, I can't be afraid to share a hard truth, but I do it to help and support my coachees. Sometimes a coaching conversation may sound confrontational to an outsider, but both parties in a strong coaching relationship know that it's not.
I'm not in management.	Coaching can be done by anyone. It's not about my level of experience or my position in the organization. All I need is a desire to help people through coaching.
My employees don't need coaching.	Just looking at employees' performance doesn't show whether they need or want it. How do I know? Have I asked? Have I considered how much more would be possible for my unit or division if team members were coached?

difficulty. She knows when a client is getting slippery or avoiding, and when the client has more to give. She has insight into what may be going on with her client that she wouldn't otherwise have."

Should you decide to become a coaching client, the best source of coaching referrals is someone who has worked with a particular coach. That kind of personal connection, however, isn't always available. Tool 2.2 provides some other resources and tips for finding your own coach. Most coaches offer free sample sessions. Take advantage of these because it's a great way to gather some tools and techniques and to see different styles of coaching.

Even if you don't choose to find a coach of your own, spend some time thinking about how you'd like to manage your gremlins. And realize that even the "best" coaches battle with gremlins from time to time.

What to Do When Your Organization Is the Obstacle

I once had a terrible job. I was doing boring work that I didn't care much about in an environment that resembled a dysfunctional family. Salespeople routinely yelled at recruiters, stole each other's clients, and made the administrators cry. At the time I wanted to be a trainer, but clearly this was not an environment that fostered learning and development. So I created opportunities for myself. I wrote a training manual for anyone new to my job (with the turnover we had, it came in handy). I offered to lead staff meetings and to train new employees. I wrote a training column for the company's national newsletter. The lesson here is that even if you are in an organization that doesn't support coaching, you can create opportunities to do at least a little bit of it. You may not be able to change your whole organization single-handedly, but usually you can change your own situation within the organization.

Worksheet 2.2 will help you identify organizations that will embrace coaching and those in which your coaching efforts will be less welcome.

TOOL 2.2

How to Find Your Own Coach

Resources

1. Visit www.coachfederation.org, the International Coach Federation's website. Click on "Find a Coach." All coaches listed there have ICF credentials certifying that they have coached a required number of hours and have been recommended by other certified coaches.

2. Accredited coaching programs listed on the ICF website likely will have their own searchable databases of graduates as well. For instance, the Coaches Training Institute maintains a referral list of coaches certified in their Co-Active coaching model. Go to www.thecoaches.com, click on "For Coaching Clients" and then click on "Find a Coach."

3. Join a coaching exchange. Find a group in which several people want to coach each other for the experience (or for a small fee). You can create one of your own exchanges or find existing ones online. Coaching & Mentoring International offers information about coaching exchanges at this page of its website: www.cmiexcel.com/uk/about/what-we-do/coaching-exchange.asp.

4. Ask someone you admire or someone who possesses qualities you aspire to possess if she would be willing to coach you.

5. Individuals in coaching certification programs are looking for clients and often are willing to charge lower-than-usual rates to log in the number of coaching hours their programs require. Contact the training programs mentioned in Step 1 to learn how to engage a coach-in-training.

Tips

Who will be the right coach for you is a personal decision. I don't believe that any selection criterion should be so rigid that it excludes someone who might be just the right fit. That said, you may want to ask a potential coach about

1. her training or certification, remembering that some coaches without any official training are exceptionally competent.

2. her background, recognizing that a background similar to your own may help you relate more easily to each other; a background different from yours can foster innovation and new ways of looking at situations you face; and a background in which she used skills you're seeking might be especially inspiring.

3. her years of experience, either as an official coach or informally in or out of the workplace.

4. her philosophy of and approach to coaching.

5. coaching results, if she has any to share. You're really hoping to hear the coach say that she doesn't promise any results. There are no guarantees in coaching, and you should be wary of people who make them.

6. any current or former clients who would be willing to talk to you about the experience of working with her.

WORKSHEET 2.2

Is My Organization the Obstacle?

Instructions: Review the list of questions and place a checkmark to the left of any to which you would answer "yes."

At your organization . . .

1. Is there a continually high-stress environment with few job perks?

2. Are big and new ideas encouraged?

3. Is there very little accountability?

4. Are there multiple opportunities for giving and receiving feedback?

5. Are new employees left to fend for themselves?

6. Does senior management seem aware of the benefits of coaching?

7. Are most performance reviews overdue?

8. Is ongoing learning and development a priority?

9. Does the organization tend to ignore, circumvent, or terminate problem employees?

10. Do good internal role models exist at all levels?

11. Is there a tendency to think it's HR's role to deal with "people" issues?

12. Is a balance of work and life encouraged?

13. Are training opportunities reserved for those at higher levels?

14. Is confrontation constructive?

15. Is turnover high?

16. Are high-potential employees recognized and provided with resources for growth?

17. Is the structure bureaucratic rather than innovative?

18. Do individuals know how they fit in and how to build a career there?

19. Has it been more than six months since your team has gone on a retreat or social outing?

20. Are there existing successful coaching relationships?

Scoring: For each checkmark you gave to an even-numbered question, give yourself one point. For each checkmark you gave to an odd-numbered question, subtract one point.

 • *If your total score falls between 7 and 10:* Your organization already embraces the growth and development of its employees. It may have a

continued on next page

coaching program in place with which you can get involved. Organiza-tions that receive a score in this range might consider introducing even more wide-ranging and innovative programs, such as periodic breakfast socials for all employees who are in a coaching pair to share their successes/lessons learned, or a training program for managers who wish to acquire coaching skills. They might be ready for monthly goal-setting support group coaching, or for group mentoring in which high-functioning divisions or departments coach those who are struggling.

• *If your total score falls between 2 and 6:* Although your organization is making headway toward becoming the learning and development organization in which coaching thrives, it may not always be far enough along for your liking. Organizations whose scores fall into this range may not decide to implement programs like coaching without some prodding, but might be willing to let a motivated individual start one. In such a case, you might want to get yourself more training in coaching because you'll need to be a role model and champion the program to get the ball rolling. Also remember tool 1.2—coaching benefits. You may want to use it to help convince senior management of coaching's merits. There's a lot in the print media right now about coaching's workplace benefits, so start a clippings file to help you build your business case for coaching.

• *If your total score is 1 or less:* It shouldn't surprise you to learn that your organization isn't fertile ground for coaching. But that doesn't mean *you* can't coach. Find one person in the organization willing to try it with you, or coach someone outside your organization—as a volunteer in the community or at another organization. An organization is motivated by results. Use the improved performance of the individual you coach to justify the coaching process, even if it runs counter to the status quo. When there's an opening for growth and development in your organization, start implementing some of the items on this worksheet (the even-numbered ones, of course) that will help create a culture that's more open to coaching. Cynicism about ideas related to employee development usually stems from lack of communication regarding what you hope to achieve and your level of commitment. Be very clear about these things and communicate them widely. Remind people that coaching is not intended to change the way people manage, but to leverage a manager's existing strengths to raise performance to an even higher level. If your organization scores in this range, I feel for you. Create a way to develop your coaching skills for as long as you want to remain with this organization.

Congratulations! By sticking to the nasty business of examining your gremlins and any unhappy aspects of your organization, you've shown your dedication to the coaching process, even in the face of real obstacles. We all have gremlins that will pop up from time to time; it's how we respond to them that will separate those of us who will progress from those who will become stuck.

Applying the Learning

◆ Can you sit still and notice? Try any of the slowing-down activities described in this step to become aware of what's present for you either in your life as a whole or specifically regarding your interest in coaching.

◆ What gremlins are you carrying with you? What do you want to do with them? Use worksheet 2.1 to become familiar with the voices trying to keep you from integrating coaching skills on the job and to figure out how you want to handle them.

◆ Have you seen any great coaches at work? Ask around and do some research to find three or four coaches with whom you can have sample sessions. You might use your coaching gremlins as a topic during the sample sessions. Even if you aren't looking for a coach in the immediate future, sample sessions can be great learning and growth experiences.

> POINTER
>
> Courage is not the absence of fear, but rather the judgment that something else is more important than fear. – *Ambrose Redmoon (aka James Neil Hollingworth), beatnik, writer, and manager of the psychedelic rock band Quicksilver Messenger Service*

◆ How ready is your organization to embrace workplace coaching? Implement some of the suggestions in the scoring section of worksheet 2.2 to garner support for coaching relationships where you work.

NOTES

_____

_____

_____

_____

_____

_____

_____

_____

_____

_____

_____

_____

_____

_____

_____

_____

_____

_____

_____

_____

_____

_____

_____

_____

Create Your Coaching Relationship(s)

OVERVIEW

How to choose your coachees

Questions for identifying a coachee's readiness

Tips for setting parameters for the relationship

Sample agreement forms to use

People's happiness, productivity, and self-esteem at work are greatly influenced by their *relationships* at work. Most of our workplace relationships, however, are haphazard. The people we surround ourselves with are those who just happen to be on our teams or in our departments; the way we interact with each other is based on existing cultural norms or assumptions; and there is very little ongoing analysis of our relationships as they progress or corrective action if they go astray.

A workplace coaching relationship is different in many ways. It's a unique relationship that requires care and attention, from choosing the right coaching partner to establishing interaction expectations. Whether formal or informal, it's a relationship that two people choose to enter together. It's a designed partnership in which the two parties make explicit decisions about how they'll interact. And it's a relationship whose "pulse" is checked continuously. Generally, the roles within a coaching relationship are defined: One person is seeking something different for herself at, or outside of, work; the other person is helping her figure out how to attain what she's seeking.

Who Will You Coach?

If you're ready to establish a coaching relationship in your workplace—if you want to use your coaching skills to accelerate the path forward for others in your organization—the first concern is how to find and enroll a coachee. How do you figure out who would benefit from a coaching relationship with you, and who would agree to do so?

Tool 3.1 presents questions to answer before selecting one or more coachees. The following sections describe how knowing the answers to those questions matters.

Await or Approach?

Some people don't need to choose whom to coach. Employees flock to their offices to tell them about their workplace issues. Employees ask them for resources, support, or advice. These people already have become informal coaches. For them, the issues are whether to limit the number of coachees they work with and what criteria to use in determining the limit.

If the profile I just gave doesn't describe you—if you want to coach others, but really don't have anyone banging down your door asking for support—you need to find coachees. For you, the issues are deciding who you want to coach and getting them to agree.

Here are three questions that might help pinpoint the people you want to approach with a coaching offer. The names you come up with in your responses aren't automatically the names of people you should be coaching; the questions are meant merely to get you thinking expansively about who might benefit from your coaching skills.

- **Is there someone who intrigues you and about whom you'd like to know more?** This is your opportunity to engage that person in more regular dialogue. If the thought of approaching that person makes you nervous, imagine how good it might feel if someone approached you and said something like, "I've always found our brief conversations in the hallway enjoyable, and I'd love to spend more time with you. I was thinking that one way to do that more regularly is if you'd be willing to be my guinea pig as I learn some new coaching skills."

◆ **Is there someone you believe could achieve better outcomes than she has achieved so far?** For example, who's been passed up for promotion, been disappointed by a response from her boss, or isn't effective at making her point

TOOL 3.1

Questions to Guide You in Choosing Coachees

	or	
Will you wait for potential coachees to approach you? *Coaching only those people who come to you with issues or questions*	or	Will you recruit/approach potential coachees? *Actively seeking employees who could benefit from your coaching*
Will you coach individuals you manage or who are in your department? *Coaching your direct reports or colleagues within your own area*	or	Will you look for coachees elsewhere in the organization? *Looking for coachees who are farther removed from your day-to-day concerns and who have less frequent contact with you*
Will you be able to coach all of your employees? *If you are a supervisor, coaching every one of the employees who report to you*	or	Will you be coaching only a chosen few? *Targeting some specific employees or starting small with just a couple of coachees*
Are you expending your coaching resources on high-potential employees? *Making coaching a perk for those who are being groomed for increased responsibilities*	or	Will you be coaching those employees who are in trouble or on the performance borderline? *Making coaching a stopgap/ last-chance intervention for employees who are not performing up to expectations*
Do you envision this as a formal coaching process? *Establishing formal coaching relationships that have specific starting and ending dates and are agreed to by both parties*	or	Will you be coaching informally? *Simply trying to be more coach-like in your day-to-day inter-actions; sneaking coaching in wherever you can*

in meetings? These are people you can approach with an opening like, "I notice that you often have your ideas shot down during meetings with senior management. I see you as a thoughtful person with really intelligent ideas. I'm learning about coaching and I think it's a tool that could help you present those ideas more powerfully. I'd be happy to talk with you more about how coaching might help you get better results."

◆ **Is there someone who's not working to her potential or seems to be stuck? Is someone's performance slipping?** These are people to approach with a message of hope: "Coaching is a tool that's helped lots of people in situations like yours. Would you be willing to try it with me?"

Worksheet 3.1 (adapted from the work of master certified life and business coach and Coaches Canada's 2007 Coach of the Year Steve Mitten) also might be a useful tool for identifying the ideal type of coachee (or the specific coachee) you'll want to approach.

Within Your Department or Elsewhere?

When I created a coaching program for managers in my last job, I required that each manager sign up with an employee partner. One of the first questions managers asked me was whether that employee should be someone who directly reported to them or someone from another department. Here are the pros and cons I shared with them at the time.

If you coach someone who actually reports to you, your return-on-investment may be higher. As you increase the performance of someone on your team, you and your team will benefit. Plus, it's part of your job as a supervisor to nurture the growth and development of your direct reports. You'll build trust and deepen your relationship with someone with whom you actually work on a daily basis, and that will improve your overall work atmosphere.

At the same time, it can be hard to go from being colleagues (or boss/report) one day to coach and coachee another. As I men-

WORKSHEET 3.1

Whom Should I Coach?

Instructions: In the first column, place the names of individuals you'd consider coaching, or groups (or types) of employees in whom you have an interest or to whom you have a connection. The middle columns present significant factors in selecting coachees. For each person or group listed in the first column, rate the factors (1 = lowest; 10 = highest). Feel free to change the factors to something more meaningful to you. Add your scores across and write the totals in the right-hand column. The totals help prioritize the various people or groups to whom you might offer your coaching services. A few examples are included.

Potential Audience or Employee	Access: It's easy to contact these people	Ease: Working with these people would be fun and free of stress	Passion: I'm energized by these people and believe I can help them excel	Competence: I have experience and interact well with people like these	Total
Senior management	9	8	4	6	27
IT staff	7	6	9	8	30
Joe J.	4	8	5	7	24
Barbara T.	8	3	4	3	18
New employees	9	10	9	6	34

tioned in Step 1, coaches shouldn't have an agenda for their coachees. If you're the coachee's direct supervisor, it can be more difficult for you to give up expectations of your employee while you're working together as coach and coachee.

To increase the likelihood of success for a coaching pair who also work together, try to go to a separate, neutral place for coaching. Draw boundaries around what role you are playing at a given moment (for example, "As your boss, I might have an answer for you, but right now I'm acting as your coach so I'd rather ask you this." or "Is there anything you need to say to me as your boss before we begin coaching today? We can spend the first five minutes of our time listing those things and then set them aside until some point in the future"). Give each other permission to point out when one person isn't sticking to his or her coach/coachee role.

When you coach someone from another department, you can offer some insight from an outsider's perspective that might not be evident to someone immersed in the situation at hand. Sometimes there is a perceived (or real) notion that the coachee can be more honest with a coach from outside her immediate area and its politics and intricacies. However, it may take longer to build trust and establish credibility with someone you don't know than it would with someone you work with. Be sure to let each other ask those "dumb" questions that people who know the technical aspects of each other's work wouldn't need to ask. When you do build that trust and credibility, new bridges often are created between departments.

There is no definite answer to the question, "Should I coach someone in my department or someone from another unit?" It's going to depend a great deal on the two people involved in the coaching relationship.

How Many or How Few?

I've seen so many well-intentioned managers who tried to be democratic by offering the same type of support to each of their employees and who ultimately gave short shrift to everyone when more pressing concerns came along. A certain amount of time and energy is required of a coach for each of his coachees—and that amount will differ according to the coach's experience, his ability to organize his time, his relationship with the coachee, and the situation the coachee is facing.

Granted, coaching should not require any work on your part outside of the coaching sessions themselves. Your role is to show up and do your best during those interactions; all preparation and assignments are the coachees' responsibility. So, depending on how many situations you can juggle or have energy for, that's how many coachees you should engage.

When you're coaching one or a few employees, especially from your own unit, there will be others who notice the attention you're paying to the coachees. They may become curious, envious, or resentful. When people don't know what's going on, they fill in the gap in information with their own worst fears or most negative assumptions. You'll want to address this matter before it produces problems in the workplace (of course, with the coachees' permission and without revealing any confidential information gathered in the coaching sessions).

The way you handle it may be as simple as a brief mention at a weekly staff meeting. It might sound something like this: "I want to let you all know that Rebecca and I are going to be working together as coach and coachee in the coming months. That's why you may see us in my office with the door closed or going out to lunch. I've been working on developing my coaching tools and I'm happy to work with any of you who have an interest in growing and developing in a particular area." Or perhaps you feel a formal description of the coaching program would be more appropriate. Example 3.1 is such a description. Caryn Siegel, of CJS Consulting, and I created this sample description for managers enrolled in a coaching workshop. Each manager went through the program with one of his or her direct reports, and we thought the managers might need some help preemptively explaining their new relationship to the rest of their team members. The sample describes the coaching

EXAMPLE 3.1

Manager "Cheat Sheet" for Participation in a Coaching Program

What Is the Coaching Program?

This series of six half-day workshops aims to improve the coaching skills of eight managers from the organization. Between workshops, the managers apply the coaching skills they've learned in one-on-one sessions with a pre-identified coachee, usually someone who actually reports to the manager on the job.

Why Is the Organization Offering This Coaching Program?

With budgets tight, the type of development that makes sense for us to invest in is development that happens on the job and is customized for the participating employee. Our coaching program is a successful example of such an investment, providing individualized development planning for employees and skills to equip managers to help employees accomplish their goals.

Other outcomes for the organization include

* decentralizing the responsibility for developing our folks
* managers with coaching abilities preventing some of the personnel issues that often find their way to HR
* strengthening the participating manager–employee pairs
* increasing productivity and morale among participating employees because they feel valued by the organization.

How Were the Participants Selected?

HR and department heads nominated manager–employee pairs to participate in the program. They were looking for pairs in which the manager has the potential to become a great coach and is very strong in other areas of management, and the employee is at a transition point in his or her career or has a goal he or she wishes to achieve. Because these sessions are for coaching rather than discipline, employees have good performance records.

Once nominated, managers and employees were told about the program. If they both left those discussions committed to participating in the program, they were accepted as one of the eight pairs.

How Can I Participate in This Program?

The coaching program will be offered again in the second quarter. If you want to participate, contact your supervisor or department head. If you meet the criteria listed below, if you have the time available, and if an appropriate partner can be found, you may be able to take part in the program. If you missed this opportunity, here are a few things you can do to be considered for the next similar opportunity:

* Tell your supervisor that this sort of opportunity is of interest to you.
* Watch the monthly employee newsletter for information about this and similar programs, including our organizationwide mentoring program that will kick off in September.

Example 3.1, continued

* Let HR know if you are looking for a professional coach or for a person to coach.

What Criteria Were Used to Select the Coachees in This Program?

We believe that coaching employees who are performing well will bring them to a level that will have a great impact on the organization. Therefore, we sought employees who

* were at a transition point in their careers and/or were considering a position of increased responsibility in the organization
* had received positive performance reviews for a two-year period prior to participation
* had an excellent attendance record
* were recommended by a supervisor, department head, or HR specialist.

What Will Be the Impact on Your Team?

Although there may be short-term inconveniences caused by having your colleagues (manager and employee) involved in workshops and coaching sessions, you all stand to benefit from this investment in the following ways:

* The job responsibilities of other team members may increase while these two people participate in the program. It's an opportunity for cross-training.
* The manager/coach has other direct reports who will benefit when the manager increases his or her ability to develop others in a customized and effective manner.

Source: Caryn Siegel and Sophie Oberstein, Redwood City coaching program.

program, why the coachee was chosen, and what the impact of their involvement might be on the team. We advised each manager/coach to share the information with her or his entire staff.

High-Potential Employee or Underperformer?

In the best-selling business book, *Good to Great: Why Some Companies Make the Leap . . . and Others Don't* (Collins Business, 2001), author Jim Collins explains that if organizations expend resources and attention on employees whose performance is fair or mediocre, they can expect those employees' performance to rise to a level that is good. From that level, employees can do better work and have better relationships. If you choose someone whose work is very good or great, you may bring that person to an exceptional level. From there, they have the opportunities to touch and affect many other people in the organization and to create many more visible and high-yield projects and programs.

So, what is your intention in choosing a coachee? Are you saving someone on the cusp of failing or being let go? Or are you bringing out the full magnificence of a highly functioning employee? Either intention is worthy of your coaching, but you really want to consider the departmental or organizational outcome you're hoping for before you decide whether you'll coach high-performing/high-potential workers or those who are not performing well.

Informal or Formal Coaching?

For any number of reasons, you may not want to create a formal coaching relationship with anyone in your organization right now. However, you still can bring coaching skills and exercises to your interactions with your co-workers. How many opportunities during a given day do you have to do this "stealth coaching"? Think about the number of meetings you attend per day; the number of phone calls you make, emails you send, performance or project reviews you facilitate; or the number of casual conversations you have. In any of those instances, you can be coach-like and make a positive difference for someone. You can use your listening skill to hear someone's state of mind, you can use your ability to give feedback, or you may ask a question that opens someone's mind to new possibilities.

What's important in informal coaching is that you remain authentic—just continue building the trusting, caring relationships at which you excel. Exploit your natural curiosity about people. People may or may not notice any difference in you when you go from unconsciously injecting coaching abilities into your interactions to doing it consciously. Have fun experimenting with new ideas and exercises. Just try slipping a question or tool from this book into an interaction with a co-worker or direct report and see how it goes.

When you're the person to whom others flock for advice and support, but you feel like what you're doing is a stretch or is

STEP 3

uncomfortable for you, transfer the responsibility. When people are asking you to go too far on their behalf or when the content of what they're sharing with you gets more troubling than you're prepared to handle, find some other people to help them. (Contact information for your organization's employee assistance plan will be handy in these situations.) And make sure that this informal coaching is something you want to be doing. Their coming to you doesn't obligate you to be their sounding board or coach. It's important that you know your limits and don't ever feel taken advantage of. You'll be doing everyone a disservice in such situations. Know who else in the organization would make a great coach for the person in front of you, and try to connect those two people.

You might decide to undertake a formal coaching process when your organization wants to implement and measure the success of such a program, when there is a widespread need for coaching organizationally (rather than just a few individuals here and there), when you need to document your efforts to help a struggling employee before letting him go, or when you're just more comfortable doing coaching in a formal context. Choosing to implement a formal coaching program will require more up-front time on the coach's part as he provides an explanation of the process and clarifies the roles of coach and coachee. Further, his sessions with the coachee will be regular, thus enabling him to plan for them rather than having them spring up on him.

It's not unheard of for a coaching relationship to be part formal and part informal. I know of one coaching pair who meets monthly as part of a more structured process and informally between those sessions. You and the coachee can design whatever creative type of relationship works for both of you.

Getting Prospective Coachees to Buy In

Regardless of the considerations you make to find a potential coachee, you need to know if she'd be interested in working with you. Example 3.2 contains some questions you might use to help a

EXAMPLE 3.2

Are You Ready for Coaching?

Coachee instructions: Respond "yes" or "no" to the following questions by putting a checkmark in the appropriate box. A person who is more open and ready for coaching will have at least five "yes" responses.

Readiness Question	Yes	No
1. Do you believe you can be more effective and happy at work?	☐	☐
2. Are you willing to consider new perspectives and try new approaches?	☐	☐
3. Do you make learning and development a priority?	☐	☐
4. Do you have some goals that keep getting pushed to the back burner?	☐	☐
5. Has someone in your life provided just the right help to you at just the right time?	☐	☐
6. Are you looking for ways to boost your career?	☐	☐
7. Are you willing to accept challenges that will move you toward your goals?	☐	☐
8. Do you want more accountability for achieving results?	☐	☐
9. Do you have a healthy attitude about receiving both positive and constructive feedback?	☐	☐
10. Do you want to work with a coach?	☐	☐

Source: Full Experience Coaching.

potential coachee consider whether this is the right time for her to embark on coaching. You can give her the questionnaire to fill out, ask her the questions in your first meeting together, or simply be on the lookout for these ideal circumstances when first talking with her.

Don't think of this questionnaire as a deal breaker, but understand that the items included are good indicators of who would respond best to coaching. They highlight whether the prospective coachee will be open to feedback and new approaches, whether she's seen similar models work, whether she's committed to coaching, and whether she recognizes an upside to the effort.

You may have to use some basic marketing tactics for approaching prospective coachees and asking them to buy in to your coaching program. Here are a few:

◆ Be yourself. Your passion and authenticity is what will draw people to you. Knowing and communicating your unique beauty and wisdom will prompt people to work with you.

◆ Use the communication method you're most comfortable with, the one that's true to who you are. If you're a writer, make your pitch via email or in a newsletter article; if you like to meet new people, use your network; if you're a talker, talk it up with everyone you meet.

◆ Do the self-awareness work first. It's hard to market yourself without carefully having identified your strengths. Do you really know what's special and valuable about you?

◆ As much as possible, make your request by explaining what's in it for the potential coachee. Rather than promoting yourself ("I'm a great coach and I'm looking for coachees"), promote what you can do for the coachee ("If you want to enhance your leadership skills, you can benefit from coaching in the following ways. . . "). Let her know what she can achieve through coaching and why it's to her advantage to do so. Use the word "you" rather than "I" when approaching your target market ("*You* will experience greater success" versus "*I* can help you"). Of course, explaining how coaching will help prospective coachees demands that you understand the needs of the people you want to reach. And remember that coaches don't promise any specific results.

◆ Educate as you market. Engaging potential coachees is a great opportunity to generate greater acceptance and understanding of coaching in the workplace and to lay the groundwork for future coaching opportunities by letting others know what coaching is all about.

◆ Tie your offer to business initiatives. Coaching for the sake of coaching is a hard sell. Coaching to groom future organization leaders or to improve the effectiveness of a current organization effort is likely to meet with more willingness.

♦ Make your message positive. People respond better to positive messages ("You'll excel with this process") than they do to negative ones ("You'll suffer without this").

♦ Remember that it can take several exposures for your offer of service to connect with your audience, and there is a fine balance between pestering potential coachees by asking too often and losing them by giving up too soon. When you really have the coachees' best interests at heart, however, a little prodding is appreciated. Clients have thanked me for sending follow-up messages or placing follow-up phone calls to make sure their desire for coaching didn't fall off the radar.

Building Your Coaching Relationship

Confidence in a relationship—particularly a coaching relationship—comes from having clear expectations and boundaries as well as from trusting that each of you knows what needs to be done and who is going to be responsible for doing it. These kinds of conversations aren't that out of the ordinary in our lives. We're all used to stating or documenting our intentions and expectations at the start of training programs, when we take a new job, when we write our wedding vows, or when we buy a home. Similar clarifying discussions should be held at the start of a coaching relationship. Tool 3.2 presents some questions you should discuss with a coachee at the beginning of your coaching relationship.

This is the time to ask your coachee what her definition of a coach is and what she most wants from you as her coach. Is she actually looking for a coach, or does she want a mentor, motivator, teacher, or guide?

And while you're all excited about working together and things are going well, you also want to talk about how to handle it when things go wrong—get this nailed down before it happens. Doing this creates an open channel of communication that will help in Step 8: Realign When Things Go Bad. And as strange as it may

TOOL 3.2

Some Questions for Initial Coaching Sessions

Expectations

* What are you hoping to achieve from coaching?

* What kind of coach do you want/need?

* What kind of coachee can I count on you to be?

* How do you envision a coaching session? What would happen during a good session?

* How much work should be done between coaching sessions? Who is responsible for completing it? What should we do if that person doesn't do what she or he committed to do?

Logistics

* How often and for how long will we meet as coach and coachee?

* Will sessions be face-to-face? Where will we meet?

* What happens if one of us can't meet and gives more than 24 hours' notice? What happens if one of us gives less than 24 hours' notice?

Troubleshooting

* What techniques will work when we hit a rough patch?

* How will we know when it's time to end the coaching relationship?

seem, you also want to talk at the beginning about the end: How will you know it's time to stop working together? How far in advance do you want to be told that coaching is about to end? (This discussion will make it easier when you reach Step 10: Complete the Coaching Cycle.)

This is also the phase in which you'll delineate your logistical expectations of each other: How much time are you committed to spending together? What happens if something else comes up on the day of your coaching appointment? What if either one of you misses more than one meeting? What if the coachee doesn't do the assignments you've agreed on? After making it clear that all plans can be adjusted as you go along, you and your coachee should agree on how often you'll meet (frequency), how long you'll meet each time (duration), where you'll meet, and when coaching will take place.

Despite everyone's best intentions, simple logistics can often ruin a good coaching relationship in the workplace. I urge you to think through what you're promising that you'll be able to do for your coaching partner. Are you committing time that you aren't sure you have? What resources and support will you need to have in place before you commit to this relationship? What other responsibilities will you have to give up, and how are you going to manage that?

For some coaching pairs, just talking about these topics will be enough. Others will want to capture their responses in writing. For those who want their agreements in print, the documents can be quite official (see example 3.3 for a contract requiring check boxes and signatures) or more descriptive and implicit (like example 3.4).

In my coaching agreements, I choose to highlight what I consider especially important in workplace coaching: the focus on the coachee, confidentiality, and upward feedback. My coaching agreement form (example 3.4) states that the client drives the coaching process. I like to make it clear from the start that the responsibility for the client's growth through this process—for success or failure—is hers. At the same time, the client is the focus of the coaching; the client does not have to ask me about my week or worry about trying to please me. When the coach is also the supervisor/manager/boss of the coachee, this permission to be self-centered is doubly important.

Confidentiality, especially when coaching is provided in a setting where you both work and associate with the same people, is going to have a big impact on the trust that you develop.

It's imperative that the coach who is also the coachee's boss give the coachee permission to give him feedback on his coaching; to tell him at any time if something is not working or if she wants to stop the coaching. He has to assure the coachee that constructive feedback will be just that, and that there will be no ramifications in other aspects of their relationship as a result of any feedback the coachee provides. Of course, this can't be empty rhetoric. This permission has to be real.

When I think of these coaching agreements, I'm reminded of an analogy from a parent educator certification program I completed.

EXAMPLE 3.3

Coaching Commitments

I, _____, (Coachee) am committed to creating a coaching alliance with _____ (Coach). The coach agrees to hold all content of our sessions completely confidential. I commit to creating a successful alliance that supports me in reaching my goals and living the life I want.

Commitment	Yes	No
I agree to participate in this coaching relationship for a minimum of three months.	☐	☐
I agree to shape the coaching relationship to best meet my needs by		
◆ sharing what I know about my own motivations.	☐	☐
◆ co-designing structures that will support me.	☐	☐
◆ asking for changes if the coaching strategy is not working.	☐	☐
I give the coach permission to		
◆ challenge me with powerful questions.	☐	☐
◆ make requests of me to take action on a goal.	☐	☐
◆ hold me accountable for taking actions to which I commit.	☐	☐
◆ speak to me in a straightforward and honest manner.	☐	☐
I agree to the following scheduling items:		
◆ If I am late for an appointment, my session will be shortened.	☐	☐
◆ I will reschedule any appointment 24 hours in advance.	☐	☐
◆ I will give one month's notice when I wish to end coaching.	☐	☐

continued on next page

Example 3.3, continued

Commitment	Yes	No
I agree to the following business arrangements:		
◆ I am entitled to two one-hour sessions per month.	☐	☐
◆ We will meet off site.	☐	☐
◆ I am entitled to unlimited email support.	☐	☐

The services to be provided by the Coach to the Coachee are coaching or tele-coaching, as jointly designed by both parties. Coaching, which is not advice, therapy, or counseling, may address specific personal projects, business successes, or general conditions in the Coachee's life or profession. Other coaching services include value clarification, brainstorming, identifying plans of action, examining modes of operating in life, asking clarifying questions, and making empowering requests.

DISCLAIMER: The Coachee is the sole decision maker in the coaching process. Any and all actions or consequences resulting from the coaching session are the responsibility of the Coachee. The Coachee releases the Coach from all liability pertaining to the services rendered in the coaching relationship.

_____

Signature of Coachee   *Date*

_____

Signature of Coach   *Date*

Source: Reprinted with permission from Meade Dickerson, Professional Executive and Life Coach, Beyond Limits, LLC.

In one study, children were observed in an outdoor setting without any fences. In that setting, the children clung to their parents and didn't venture far from where their parents sat. Other children were observed in a large fenced area. There the children explored every nook and cranny inside the fence and didn't necessarily stay close to their parents. These agreements are like the fence that provides the protection and comfort for coachees to venture to the outer edges of what's possible from this coaching relationship.

STEP **3**

EXAMPLE 3.4

Coaching Agreements

Becoming a coaching client is making a commitment to your own growth. It is also a commitment between you and another person, your coach. You are the driver of this coaching process. The following agreements spell out our commitments to each other and will serve as the basis for the coaching relationship we are entering. I am committed to helping you become more fulfilled in all of the arenas of your life—your full experience.

Our focus	The focus of this coaching is you. You create the agenda we will follow. You complete the inquiries and assignments that we agree on. This is a time to be "self-full" and to center solely on what you are needing and feeling. Don't worry about pleasing me as your coach or asking me about myself. Get comfortable with this being about you alone. Additionally, know that coaches do not give advice or make promises about outcomes— what you get from this coaching is directly aligned with what you put into it.
Confidentiality	Our relationship is completely confidential. I will not be telling anyone you are my client and I will not reveal the content of our coaching sessions to anyone. This is true even when your coaching is being paid for by your employer. You are free to share whatever you choose from our sessions with anyone. I do request permission to report your name and contact information to the International Coach Federation for ongoing certification purposes.
Feedback	Periodically, I will ask for feedback on my coaching, and I welcome this type of feedback at any time. If I ever do or say anything that upsets you or doesn't feel right, please bring it to my attention. I promise to make it right for you and do what is necessary to have you be satisfied.
Time commitment	Although coaching can address a short-term issue or a decision that needs to be made, the ideal commitment to the coaching process is approximately four months. That is enough time to establish a relationship, to experience success, and to work through failures. It means that if the going gets tough, you will stick with it long enough to see results. After the initial four-month period, you can continue on a month-to-month basis. That said, some clients go month-to-month from the start, some make a one-year commitment at the start, or agree to any other span of time they believe is workable.

continued on next page

Sessions	Coaching sessions are 45 minutes, three times per month. At the end of each month, we will select three dates for the following month. Ideally, we will lock in a time that works consistently for both of us. With very few exceptions, sessions are conducted by phone.
Timeliness	Please call me at our pre-designated time. If I do not hear from you by 15 minutes after our appointed time, I will have to charge you for the time I have set aside in my day for your session. If ever you call me and I do not answer, please leave a message. If I don't call you back within 10 minutes, your next session is free.
Payment	At the beginning of each month, you will receive an invoice for payment. Prompt payment is appreciated.
Rescheduling	If you need to reschedule, I would appreciate 24 hours' notice. I will do all I can to reschedule within the same week. In our busy lives, each of us occasionally will need to move a session. I will extend to you the same courtesy and give you as much notice as possible when something comes up for me. If we are unable to reschedule a session that you have already paid for, we will bank the session and your invoice the following month will reflect that.
Extra coaching	Call me between our scheduled sessions if you need a sounding board, have a problem, or want to share a success with me. I have time between our regular sessions to speak with you, if needed, and I enjoy providing this extra level of service. I do not bill for additional time of this type, but ask that you keep the extra sessions to less than 10 minutes. Also, contact me by email as often as you'd like.
Completing our relationship	When either one of us decides it is time to end our coaching relationship, we should advise the other person of our decision when we have at least two coaching sessions remaining. This will give us time to capture your learning and strategize for what is next in your life.

These agreements are not all-inclusive. Coaching is a dynamic and personalized process. If something you've just read needs to be revised to make you comfortable, we can do that. As other situations arise, we will find a mutually satisfying way of handling them. These agreements are simply the foundation of something that has yet to be built. I'm looking forward to creating that something with you.

Source: Full Experience Coaching.

STEP 3

We humans are social animals and our relationships are very important to us. A workplace coaching relationship has the potential to be one of those transforming and positive relationships in our lives. It deserves our thoughtful attention here, where we have the chance first to create it and thereafter to nurture it.

Applying the Learning

◆ What kind of coaching relationship works for you? Have you weighed the pros and cons of each of the considerations in tool 3.1?

◆ Who is your target audience? Who do you want to coach? Can you approach someone in that population right now and offer her the opportunity to work with you? If she's unsure about whether she's ready to work with a coach, run through some of the questions included in example 3.2.

◆ What agreements do you need to have in place? Look over the sample agreement forms to see what's in them that you'd need in your coaching agreements. Sit with your coachee and ask her what she needs or expects from you. If it helps, have tool 3.2 nearby during this conversation.

◆ In what way do you need to behave differently when you are coaching your coachee than when you are working with or managing her? Have you been explicit with her about how you intend to keep these roles delineated?

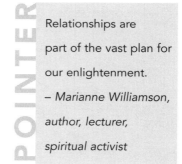

Relationships are part of the vast plan for our enlightenment.

– Marianne Williamson, author, lecturer, spiritual activist

N O T E S

_____
_____
_____
_____
_____
_____
_____
_____
_____
_____
_____
_____
_____
_____
_____
_____
_____
_____
_____
_____
_____
_____
_____

Find Out About Your Coachee

OVERVIEW

Discussion of personality typing

What input to gather and how to do it

How to conduct personal observations

How to uncover your coachee's values, skills, and accomplishments

It took a tragedy in our workplace—a premature death—for us to learn the intricate details of the life of one of our colleagues (whom I'll call Vince). We'd known Vince as a quiet person and a hard worker, someone who was often at work late into the night. You could always turn to Vince for help with a project. We knew he was married and had adult children. I spoke with his department head shortly after Vince's funeral, and he told me, "Vince was always an enigma. I didn't know him until I heard his family and friends talking about him at his funeral. They shared personal things about him and his interests that I was surprised to learn." How much could our relationship with him have been deepened had we all known these things about him? How much more effective could his supervisor have been if he'd known what drove Vince and what he'd always longed for? What could we have done to tie his interests to the work at hand? Why didn't we ask him these types of questions when we had the chance?

I hope that no one else has to have this experience or to live with regret about not getting to know a co-worker, and I encourage all colleagues to be curious about each other. When you're a coach, it's not just nice to find out these types of things about your coachee; it's critical to the process. In the service of your coachee's goals and dreams, you want to know what makes him tick. Who is he at his core? Who is he when he's annoyed or when he gets stressed with multiple deadlines? What brings him joy?

For several reasons you want this information early in a coaching relationship. By showing the coachee you care about getting to know him, you continue to build trust and rapport. By finding out what drives him, you know how to motivate and encourage him when times are tough. By knowing his strengths and past accomplishments, you can offer genuine feedback about who he is and what he's capable of. When setting goals (Step 5), you'll know what really will excite him and what he's most likely to do.

What's often surprising is how much coachees learn about themselves while you're discovering all you can about them. Often, they've never been asked in the workplace the questions you'll ask, and the simple act of articulating and noticing their responses can produce positive changes for them.

Finally, when you set aside time for your coachee to learn more about himself, you'll avoid the types of issues that I mentioned in the preface—participants showing up for training programs without a context to take in all that they were going to learn. The individuals to whom training didn't stick were those who'd never explored their own needs, career paths, or interests. When your coachee has done some self-exploration, the coaching to follow will be more effective and meaningful.

Personality Typing

Many coaches begin to understand their coachees by having them complete some sort of personality typing instrument or profile at the start of their coaching relationship. According to Matt Ahrens, organizational development consultant and the founder of Solution

Points, such tools are helpful in describing some typical behavior patterns and stumbling blocks for different types of people. Knowing these personality patterns helps you anticipate where your coachee might get hung up or what blocks might get in his way. And you can learn some of the strengths typically tied to his personality type. Sometimes it's reassuring to a coachee who is experiencing some trouble when you recognize the struggle as something typical of his personality type rather than some unique shortcoming. That allows him to look at the situation more dispassionately. Also, asking a coachee who's stuck to look at his situation from the vantage point of a different personality type can help him see things from a fresh perspective.

There are hundreds of personality inventories available. Some of the more popular ones are the Myers-Briggs Type Indicator, DISC, the Social Style Model, the Enneagram, and the Herrmann Brain Dominance Instrument. More subject-specific profiles also can be useful—for example, Situational Leadership and SkillScope, which measure leadership competencies.

A typing metric that I particularly like is one that identifies the coachee's learning style. It's important for a coachee to know if he enjoys and learns through self-reflection and working alone (intrapersonal) or through group relationships and communication (interpersonal). Does he need information presented via visual images and pictures (visual/spatial), through numbers (logical/mathematical), or written and spoken words (verbal/linguistic)? Is he a "body smart" person who learns through action and body memory (kinesthetic), or does he recognize tonal patterns and learn through rhythm and repetition (musical)?

Whichever personality typing instrument you use, Ahrens says it's most critical to reinforce with your coachee that a person is not merely his personality type. He cautions us to remember that we're all individuals. Our essence lays "beneath that pattern of thinking, feeling, and behaving that the instrument measures. Don't assume you know someone better than they know themselves simply because of their type."

Many of these instruments require you to be certified or licensed to administer, score, and interpret them. However, there are several ways to work with profiles even if you aren't certified:

◆ Partner with someone who is certified to administer and analyze instrument results. Just make sure that you, the administrator, and the coachee have agreed on the roles each of you will play and the confidentiality parameters you want to have in place. Will you sit in on the interpretation session? Will you and the administrator discuss the coachee's results with or without him present? Do you have his permission to do so? Your coachee can get a lot of value from this typing process, even if you're not directly involved.

◆ Pick an instrument and share with your coachee the instrument's descriptions of each of the different personality types or preferences. (You can find these online or in books about each typing instrument.) Let your coachee choose the personality type to which he most relates. Of course, this isn't a scientific approach, but because the coachee knows himself better than anyone else knows him, he's very likely to pick the type that best describes him. Ahrens always gives coachees a choice of two personality types. "I think you're this type," he might say, "but you also may want to consider this closely related one."

◆ Many coachees have completed one or more personality profiles in the past. I've met people who've had the results of several of them tucked away in their desk drawers. Ask your coachee to bring in the results of profiles he's completed previously, and use these results as the basis of a conversation.

You don't need to have new coachees complete a personality profile because there are many other ways to uncover their essence, abilities, and desires. But using a tried-and-true tool like a personality inventory can give you a quick snapshot of a person's preferences and style.

Input from Others

Coaching relationships can start off with the coach collecting information about the coachee from other people. The coach might ask the coachee to identify a variety of people he comes in contact with at work—or even, in some cases, outside of work—from whom the coach can get information about the coachee.

There are several situations where soliciting input from others would be beneficial: When coaching's been requested to address a specific performance-related issue, the coach may need more information on the weakness the coachee's boss has noticed or the results the organization expects from the coachee. If a coachee wants to set a particular goal that his boss doesn't consider important, it's good to know the boss's feelings before the coachee spends too much energy on an unimportant goal. By getting input from the boss at the start of coaching, you and the coachee learn which goals are realistic and valuable to the boss and to the organization.

Another person's perspective adds dimension to a discussion or gives the coachee the impetus for working on something he didn't previously see as an issue. Outside input is also useful when the coachee is working on a particular issue that hasn't been covered in prior performance evaluations or when he's being groomed for, or has been passed over for, a promotion.

When an organization is paying for coaching, it sometimes expects the coach to consult with the coachee's boss at regular intervals, including at the start of the relationship.

You can collect data from the coachee's boss, direct reports, and co-workers at informal meetings. A very simple format for these meetings is asking about the coachee's strengths, weaknesses, opportunities, and threats (a SWOT analysis).

POINTER

It is important when you've been asked to coach an employee by his boss that you clarify with the boss just who your "client" will be. To whom are you responsible? To whom do you communicate? Will you report coaching results to the boss, or is it the coachee who will share any information he wishes to with the boss?

Another option is to use a formal 360-degree feedback instrument to gather data from a variety of people. Although standardized 360-degree tools are broadly available, it sometimes is more relevant to create your own. Although it's more labor intensive (that is, you'll have to tally the results yourself and look for themes to share with the coachee), creating your own instrument lets you ask about qualities or categories that are meaningful to your coachee and the organization.

Example 4.1 is a 360-degree feedback survey I created when I worked for Redwood City. It asks people to rate the coachee on competencies tied to the organization's values. Surveys also may be based on leadership competencies, job descriptions, or the specific items the coachee feels he should be working on or on which he'd like more detailed feedback. Use the example as a template for your own 360-degree input-gathering instrument.

Whatever type of instrument you use, be certain that it ensures confidentiality for the coachee and for those offering input about him. Make sure that the coachee and the raters know how the data will be used. (Of course, that means *you* need to know that you have a reason for putting the coachee through the experience and what you're going to do with the data.) Make it clear to the raters that the coachee won't see their individual comments and that they (the raters) won't see a report of the feedback collected (unless the coachee chooses to share it with them). Explain that the input is only for the coachee's development.

You don't always have to get input from others to find out about your coachee, but doing so can provide another perspective on the issues he faces and where he should be focusing his earliest coaching efforts. When you compare the responses of others with those provided by the coachee, you also get some insight on how self-aware he is.

EXAMPLE 4.1

360-Degree Feedback Survey

Coachee instructions:

1. Decide whose ratings you would like to include in your survey and ask those people if they would be willing to participate as raters.
   - Select five to eight raters.
   - Your direct supervisor should be one of the raters.
   - The remaining raters may be your direct reports, your peers, or other managers in the organization.
   - Raters may be from your department or another.
2. Submit your raters' names on the rater form below.
3. Write your name on the top of each of the surveys you will be handing out.
4. Give each rater an instruction sheet and survey.
5. Tell the raters to return the surveys to HR by April 15.

360-DEGREE FEEDBACK SURVEY RATER FORM

Please return this form to HR by April 1.

Your name: _____

Rater	Relationship to You (Boss, Peer, Direct Report)	How Long Have You Known This Rater?

continued on next page

STEP 4

Example 4.1, continued

Rater instructions:

Thank you for agreeing to complete this survey. By doing so you have the opportunity to help the person who gave it to you learn more about his or her strengths, as well as areas where development may be needed.

Please be candid in providing feedback and include examples in the comments section that illustrate your ratings. We encourage your honesty and completeness. This is the place for objective performance observations. Be assured that your answers will be completely anonymous; they always will be combined with others and never will be identifiable in any way. Please return the completed survey to HR by April 15. If you have questions as you are completing the survey, you can contact Sophie at x5956 or via email.

Thank you for your input!

360-DEGREE FEEDBACK SURVEY RATER FORM

Please return this form to HR by April 15.

Name of person being rated:

Part 1. Rate the participant on the 22 competencies listed on the left-hand side by circling the appropriate number on the right.
Legend: **1** = Is Poor at it   **2** = Is Fair at it   **3** = Is Good at it   **4** = Excels at it

Competency	Rating			
Community Building				
Effective communication with diverse individuals and groups	1	2	3	4
Relationship building	1	2	3	4
Sensitivity	1	2	3	4
Building team spirit	1	2	3	4

Competency	Rating			
Excellence				
Using the strengths of others to get things done	1	2	3	4
Providing autonomy to employees	1	2	3	4
Inclusion (doesn't play favorites or exclude anyone)	1	2	3	4

Excellence

Administrative organizational ability	1	2	3	4
Leading by example	1	2	3	4
Coping with pressure	1	2	3	4
Time management	1	2	3	4

Integrity

Professionalism	1	2	3	4
Accountability	1	2	3	4
Asking for participation from staff on decisions, projects	1	2	3	4
Knowing and accepting his/her own strengths and limitations	1	2	3	4

Service

Approachability (you feel welcome and listened to)	1	2	3	4
Energy, drive, ambition	1	2	3	4
Technical expertise	1	2	3	4
Results-orientation	1	2	3	4

Creativity

Innovation	1	2	3	4
Analysis	1	2	3	4
Flexibility	1	2	3	4

Part 2. Answer the following two questions about the participant's greatest strength and his or her challenges. Strengths and challenges might include any of the competencies listed in Part 1 (for example, highly innovative or lacking in sensitivity) or they might be other talents or characteristics you've noticed in the participant. Please include descriptions or comments to explain the terms you use.

This person's **greatest asset** is . . . .

What **challenges** does this person have to overcome to be more effective?

STEP

4

continued on next page

Example 4.1, continued

Part 3. Circle the appropriate response in the left-hand column and give an explanation in the right-hand column.

Statement	Explanation
I would happily work for this person: a. Strongly agree b. Agree c. Disagree e. Strongly disagree	Why would or wouldn't you like to work for this person?
This person works best with [circle as many as apply]: a. His/her colleagues b. His/her boss c. His/her team members/direct reports d. Other: _____	Why do you feel this person works best with the group(s) you identified?

Source: Sophie Oberstein, Redwood City Succession Planning Program.

Making Observations

Sometimes the most powerful way to learn about your coachee's style and impact is to observe him at work. Ask to sit in on his regular staff meeting or a project meeting to see how others respond to him, what impression he gives, and how he communicates. Or set yourself up in your coachee's office for two hours to watch how he uses his time, how he handles interruptions, or how many times the phone rings.

Before you begin your on-site observations, work with your coachee to plan how he's going to position your presence for his staff. I usually guide my clients to say something like this: "I'm working with a coach to improve my presentation skills. Next week, my coach wants to sit in on our staff meeting and I want to make sure that's OK with all of you. You should know that she is only here to watch me and to give me some feedback on my presentation skills; she won't be watching or grading you. Our ideas aren't being evaluated, and no one but me is getting any feedback from this ob-servation. Please let me know in the next day or two if this will be a problem for you. Otherwise, I'll assume it's OK to have her here."

Also before you observe your coachee in action, let him know that he should be himself, that trying to impress you or be differ-ent than he usually is only cheats him of real learning. Tell him not to prepare more for this meeting than any other meeting. Have him create a signal he can use if he needs you to leave the meeting— for example, if something heated or confidential comes up, or if he gets uncomfortable or senses someone else in the room is growing uncomfortable. When you see the signal, leave. Just knowing he has this option usually is enough to make him feel safe. Make sure you know ahead of time the context you'll be observing him in and if there is anything in particular he wants you to be watching for.

As soon after the observation as possible, sit with the coachee and give him your feedback. An effective model for delivering your input is the "sandwich" model—one piece of constructive feedback sandwiched between a few positives or strengths. Give the coachee an opportunity to respond to the feedback both immediately and after some time has passed.

If it's impossible for you to observe his actions in person, you might have him video- or audiotape meetings (with the permission of the people in the room). This may be preferable to a personal observation because it enables you to play back his actions when you're delivering feedback so that he sees or hears them for himself.

Observing can be a regular part of workplace coaching and isn't limited to this step in the process. In fact, if you do it at regular intervals throughout the coaching process, it can provide dramatic evidence of results. Plus, there really is no better way to make positive improvements than to get feedback based on a direct observation of ourselves in action.

Feedback Basics

As you can see from this discussion of observation as a coaching tool, giving feedback is a key competency for the effective coach. If it's been a while since you reviewed the basics of feedback, here are eight elements that you'll need to make part of your feedback process:

1. Feedback is most effective when it has been **solicited.** When you have feedback for someone who hasn't asked for it, it's important to ask for permission before delivering it to make sure that your coachee is ready to hear it and won't react defensively. In coaching, you get this permission at the start of the relationship and generally don't need to ask again each time you have something to share.

2. Feedback should be **immediate.** It's important to deliver feedback as soon after the observed behavior as possible, primarily so that the coachee will remember the action or situation to which you're referring.

3. Feedback must be **specific.** It's an objective, detailed reflection of what you've seen or heard the coachee do.

4. Feedback often addresses the observed behavior's **impact** on you or others. Such feedback might sound like this: "When you come back from lunch 5 minutes late, I have to remain at the front desk and I'm late to my next meeting. That's really embarrassing for me." This type of feedback rarely elicits a defensive reaction because it's hard for someone to argue that you didn't experience something (embarrassment, in the example given) that you're saying you did experience.

5. When possible, feedback should be **balanced.** Not always negative and not always positive. One caveat to this desired balance: feedback, above all, should be **genuine,** so don't force yourself to add something good or bad if there isn't anything good or bad to share.

6. Constructive feedback should be **actionable.** It might suggest a plan for changing the coachee's behavior in the future and for following up on progress.

7. Constructive feedback should be **achievable,** addressing aspects of the coachee's behavior or characteristics that are within his control. Giving feedback on someone's accent, height, or boss, for example, is counterproductive because these aren't things the coachee can change.

8. After delivering feedback, it's a good idea to allow the recipient to **respond.** What's his perspective on the situation, or on your feedback? Some recipients will need time to reflect on, or to process, what you've shared. Let the coachee know when and how he can come back to you for clarification or further comment. It's a good idea to ask him to check back in with you, not only to share how he's feeling about the feedback, but also to share how he has implemented your suggestion.

Here's how a piece of feedback that incorporates many of those elements might sound: "Carl, may I give you some feedback on your interaction with that angry customer (*solicited*) who just left (*immediate*)? [Wait for response.] I noticed that the customer's voice got louder when you repeatedly used the phrase, 'I know just how you feel' *(specific)*. Did you notice she was yelling, 'You don't know how I feel—how could you possibly know how I feel?' *(impact/asking for response)*. May I suggest a response that's less likely to get that kind of reaction from an angry customer *(solicited)*? [Wait for response.] How about using an apology, not for causing the situation but for the situation she's in, like, 'I'm sorry this happened to you' *(suggestion)*. Would you be willing to try that next time and tell me how it goes *(asking for response)*?"

Identifying Values

STEP

4

People experience fulfillment when their actions and behavior honor the values they hold. This confluence of values and actions is so critical to getting effective performance from your employees and to having a motivated workforce that I'm going to say it again, inserting a few work-related phrases: Employees experience fulfillment in their jobs (which then translates to happiness in their jobs and increased productivity) when what they do at work on a daily basis honors the values they hold.

Some people say that values stay constant over time; that they are what lies in the coachee's essence, even when other aspects of his personality may change. I'm not sure I agree. I think that some of the principles that are important to me as a middle-aged person were far less important to me when I was fresh out of college. For example, ambition was a value for me then; peace (which I never would have included in a list of my values during my college years) overrides that now.

POINTER

There can be no happiness if the things we believe in are different from the things we do. – *Freya Madeline Stark, travel writer*

In a coaching context, a value is whatever is important to the coachee—whatever he wouldn't want to live without. I don't analyze whether something a coachee tells me is important to him is, strictly speaking, a value. If he says, "The hiking trail behind my house is so important to me I couldn't imagine life without it," I list "hiking trail" as one of his values.

Then I'll ask him to explain what that hiking trail brings up for him, and he might say, "Nature, physical activity, tranquility, and no stress." Now we're getting closer to his values, in the traditional sense of the word. Physical objects may suggest a person's values, and digging a little deeper can reveal the values that underlie the desires for specific objects.

When doing values exercises, you want to be expansive at first, listing as many values as you can think of or as many as you can coax out of the coachee. Don't critique or question each one. Then prioritize the list. Prioritizing values is a real process of discovery for coach and coachee alike.

One very simple way to start the conversation about values is to talk together about the organization's values and what those mean to the coachee. Then explore how the coachee's personal values resonate with those of the team, department, or organization. This is a clear way to link what the employee is doing on the job with what he believes it is important for him to do in the world.

Another way to highlight work-related values is to ask the coachee to close his eyes and think about a time when he was completely excited by his work, when he woke up eager to get out of bed and into the office, when he didn't even care whether he was getting paid to do what he was doing. This time doesn't have to be recent. It doesn't have to be in his current job. And it doesn't have to be dramatic. It can be a simple moment when he just felt content at work. Ask him to see that time clearly; to notice what was going on around him, how he was feeling, who else was there, and so forth. When he opens his eyes, ask him to share what he saw. Jot down those things he shares that clearly are important to him in a work situation. Check your list with him afterward to make sure that he agrees with what you heard as his values, and that you didn't leave anything big off the list.

Here are a few other ways to discern the coachee's values:
◆ Have the coachee write down all of the different ways he identifies himself—for example, father, teacher, mechanic, Catholic, coffee drinker, yoga enthusiast, and the like.

Then ask him to pick the five descriptors that are most important and to tell you about them.

- ◆ Give him a disposable camera and ask him to take photos of the things that are important in his life. As an alternative, simply ask him to bring in a dozen photos of those things.
- ◆ Meet at a site that is important to your coachee and ask him to give you a tour and tell you about its significance in his life.
- ◆ Use a checklist of values from which he can choose those that are most important to him. Generally, this isn't an option I favor because no list is complete and, in this case, the list can shape perception. But there is one values survey I do like (example 4.2). It was created by Christine Bennett and WorkVantage Inc., an organizational development and training firm.

So, when working with values, follow this process:

1. Be expansive and list on paper as many words or phrases that have meaning to the coachee as you can.

2. Ask him to choose the four to six phrases about which he feels most strongly.

3. For each of the selected values, have him really bring it to life for you. Ask questions like, What does this value mean to you? What other words describe this value? How does it make you feel? What's happening when you're living this value?

4. Ask questions that reveal to what extent the coachee currently is honoring each value in his work (or life) and what he can do to reach a place where he is more in alignment with it. Here are a couple of sample questions: On a scale of 1 to 10, how much are you honoring this value today? What can you do right now to move closer to honoring this value every day?

EXAMPLE 4.2

Clarifying Values

Coachee instructions: For each of the values listed on the left, indicate its level of importance by placing a checkmark in one of the columns to the right. Don't think too long about each one because your first reactions are often the most accurate. When you've completed the survey, identify the five values that are most important to you and write a short definition of what that value means in your life.

Action values: "I would like to ..."	Unimportant	Not very important	Important	Critical
Create ideas				
Make things				
Fix things				
Help people				
Design systems				
Perform physical tasks				
Organize things				
Create beauty				
Explore ideas				
Follow directions				
Take responsibility				
Experience variety				
Improve society				
Laugh often				
Take risks				
Be in nature				
Manage people				
Work in teams				
Other:				

Result values: "I would like to have..."	Unimportant	Not very important	Important	Critical
Achievement				
Beauty around me				
Knowledge				
Pleasure				
Power				
Recognition				

continued on next page

STEP **4**

Example 4.2, continued

Result values: "I would like to have..."	Unimportant	Not very important	Important	Critical
Wealth				
Adventure				
Comfort				
Independence				
Leisure time				
Possessions				
Simplicity				
Security				
Structure/order				
Stability				
Wisdom				
Family harmony				
Friendship				
Self-respect				
Inner harmony				
Integrity				
Equality				
Love				
Other:				

Personal quality values: "I want to be..."	Unimportant	Not very important	Important	Critical
Generous				
Fulfilled				
Healthy				
Moral				
Physically attractive				
Spiritual				
Ambitious				
Caring				
Cooperative				
Disciplined				
Positive				
Needed				
Happy				

STEP 4

Example 4.2, continued

Personal quality values: "I want to be . . . "	Unimportant	Not very important	Important	Critical
Efficient				
Open-minded				
Competent				
Logical				
Sensitive				
Creative				
Fair				
Environmentally aware				
Honest				
Other:				

My Top Five Values	What this value means to me
1.	
2.	
3.	
4.	
5.	

Source: Used with permission of Christine Bennett, WorkVantage Inc.

Identifying Skills and Achievements

What someone has achieved in the past is often a good indicator of what he can achieve in the future. When times get tough, however, coachees often forget all of the great things they've accomplished. As a coach, you can collect these achievements and, when necessary, remind the coachee of them. Focusing on achievements and skills that come naturally to the coachee also helps identify what work or projects would be a good fit for him.

Here are some activities you can complete to determine the coachee's achievements and skills.

◆ Ask the coachee to list eight to 10 specific accomplishments or projects by which he has demonstrated some degree of skill, achieved a goal, or explored a new challenge. Be sure he is specific when describing his accomplishments. As an example, you're looking for things like "I published an article in our trade magazine," not "writing." In a similar exercise, Christine Bennett recommends that coachees include the accomplishments that made *them* feel good, not those that others praised them for; and she reminds them to include all segments of their lives, not just their work. After they've listed these accomplishments, there are several things you can do with them: Notice the themes in the list. Identify the skills necessary to have achieved them, and explore how much the coachee is using those skills today. Or, ask him to rank his accomplishments and their related skills in descending order of importance.

◆ Ask the coachee to write the text someone would use to introduce him as he was about to deliver a presentation to his colleagues. What would the introduction highlight about him and his background?

◆ Richard Nelson Bolles' classic book *What Color Is Your Parachute?* includes several exercises that help individuals identify their skills and accomplishments. Some coaches structure all of their sessions around a particular book of exercises like that one.

◆ Complete an exercise. For example, if your coachee identifies one of his core skills as training, have him train you for 20 minutes. If it's writing, have him write something. Accounting? Have him audit some numbers.

◆ Pull out old performance evaluations and look for themes.

◆ Use questions like these in your initial coaching sessions:

   ◆ Which assignments or roles in the past provided you with the most challenge? The least? Why?

   ◆ What accomplishment are you most proud of, and why?

   ◆ What part of your education or work experience has been the most valuable to you over the years?

   ◆ What actions have you taken to manage your career?

   ◆ What lessons have you learned from your successes or failures?

- What is your biggest challenge in trying to balance your work and personal life?
- What do you want to accomplish before you die?
- What do you think your co-workers say about you when you're not around?

Example 4.3 is a skills analysis of the type that you may want to use with your coachee. Any exercise that asks the coachee to identify and sort his existing skills is useful. What I most like about this example is that it helps you and your coachee identify a few categories of skills: **Core skills** are those in which he is highly proficient and takes total delight or very much enjoys using. Knowing his core skills is helpful in coaching because these are the skills he can rely on when you're pushing him to try new things. **Wish-list skills** are those he delights in or very much enjoys using, but in which he has little or no skill. These are skills he should focus on to accomplish new and desired outcomes. **Ball-and-chain skills** are those he's highly proficient in but prefers not to use or strongly dislikes. As a coach, you'll want to help your coachee restructure

STEP **4**

EXAMPLE 4.3

Analyzing Job Skills

Coachee instructions: Create a list of skills you use in your job. Then copy each one into the appropriate box on the chart below, considering both how much you enjoy using that skill and how competent you are at it. It's okay to have more than one skill in any box.

	Highly Proficient	Competent	Little or No Skill
Totally delight in using			
Enjoy using very much			
Like using			
Prefer not to use			
Strongly dislike using			

Source: This example is based on the work of Richard Knowdell. It is used with permission of WorkVantage.

his time so that he's using these skills at work less than 15–20 percent of his time.

Discovery Forms and Fun Questions

Discovery forms are tools that coaches use to facilitate the learning part of this step. These forms are places where coachees may write their responses to questions prior to a coaching session and where the coach can get a peek at the coachee's values and personality before or between sessions. They're good jumping-off places for initial coaching discussions. There are many different types of discovery forms that include many different types of questions. As a sample, I've included the discovery form I use with my new clients (example 4.4), and one created by Ben Dooley, a coach who works with other coaches (example 4.5).

Not all questions you pose during the discovery phase of coaching need be serious or work-related. You can learn a lot about a person by how he responds to some questions that are just plain curious or fun. Not only do you learn from the content of his responses, but you also learn about his creativity and his willingness to play (important aspects of your working relationship). If the two discovery forms provided here don't include enough fun questions for you, here are a few more:

♦ If you could hear a speech from the leading figure in any field, who would you choose to hear?

♦ What is the longest walk you've ever taken?

♦ What would a movie about your life be called? Who would play you? What songs would be on the soundtrack?

♦ What would a stained glass window in your home/office depict?

♦ If you could add one piece of furniture to your office, what would it be?

♦ What one object should you throw away—but never will?

♦ You've just been given a chance to host your own talk show. What will make your show unique?

EXAMPLE 4.4

Discovery Form A

Thank you for becoming my client! I look forward to working with you to bring a higher level of fulfillment to your life.

In coaching, we often call our initial conversations "discovery" sessions. These are conversations that enable me to discover who you are and let you experience self-discovery. There are three main objectives to these discussions: (1) to learn about who you are, (2) to create a compelling vision for the future, and (3) to design how we can best work together.

The questions below help illuminate some of these areas. You may need some time to consider your answers. Please come to the first session prepared to discuss as many of them as you can. Either think about them, jot down some notes about them, or (better yet) send me your random thoughts about them prior to our first session so we can use them as a jumping-off point for our discussion.

Please note that you need only respond to the questions that attract you. Answer as many or as few as you like. Try not to be restricted by the size of the response box. Write as much or as little as you desire.

Part One—About Me

1. What does my coach really need to know about me (and how I make changes) that will help her most in coaching me?

2. What is my greatest gift?

3. What am I most challenged by?

4. What is my unique contribution/passion?

5. What activities have heart and meaning for me?

6. What brings me joy?

continued on next page

7. If I could add any course to the nation's school curriculum, what would it be?

8. If I could add one room to my current home, what would it be?

9. Who are two people who inspire me? Why?

STEP 4

10. What's my dream?

Part Two—A Compelling Vision

1. What are the three biggest changes I want to make in my life/career in the next three years?

2. What's missing in my life that would make it more fulfilling?

3. If time and resources weren't issues, what things would I want to do?

4. If this coaching were to have a huge impact on my life, what would that impact look like?

Part Three—My Coaching Needs

1. More than anything else, what do I want from my coach, and from the coaching relationship?

2. What is my biggest doubt about coaching and how do I think coaching might (or might not) help me?

3. What can my coach do or say when I'm most "stuck" that will return me to action?

4. What do I think about "homework"? How much of it do I want between sessions? Do I want each session to start with a check-in on homework? What should my coach do if I don't complete the homework?

STEP 4

Part Four—Prior Self-Discovery

Here is a description of other self-discovery work I have done (or am currently doing):

Note: This might include other coaching, therapy, seminars, personality typing, and so forth. Knowing this enables us to integrate what you've already done with what we are embarking on together. If you've already developed vision, mission or life purpose statements, values, or goals, please send along whatever you're comfortable sharing.

Source: Full Experience Coaching.

EXAMPLE 4.5

Discovery Form B

Coachee instructions: Please complete this form to the best of your ability and return it to me. (Don't worry about items you leave blank. We'll fill them in as coaching proceeds.)

Name:

Over the next three years, what are the three biggest changes you want to make in your life so that you will be on a path to living a life with no regrets?

1.

2.

3.

If there were a secret passion in your life, what would that be?

What would you say have been your three greatest accomplishments?

1.

2.

3.

What is the hardest thing you have had to overcome in your life?

What major transitions have you made in the past two years (new decade of life, new relationship, new job, new role, new residence, and so forth)?

Have you worked with a coach (or been in therapy) before? If so, what worked well for you and what did not?

Who are the key people in your life, and what do they provide you?

What's missing in your life? What would make it more fulfilling?

What are you learning/accepting about yourself at present?

Rate the amount of stress in your life right now (1 = low, 10 = high).

What are your primary stressors?

List five things that you are tolerating in your life right now:
1.
2.
3.
4.
5.

List five adjectives that describe you at your best:
1.
2.
3.
4.
5.

List five adjectives that describe you at your worst:
1.
2.
3.
4.
5.

What motivates you?

What are your three major concerns/fears about yourself?
1.
2.
3.

continued on next page

STEP 4

What are your three major concerns/fears about life?

1.

2.

3.

What would you like me to do when you get behind in your goals? How do you like to be held accountable?

Do you have a personal or professional vision? If so, what is it?

What would you like to contribute to the world?

What dream or goal have you given up?

If you continue to live as you do, what regrets will you have?

Source: Adapted and used with the permission of Ben Dooley.

◆ You've won $50,000 and have to give it all to charity. Which charity will you choose?

◆ Who are the top five to 10 people you regard as all-time-great Americans?

◆ If you could have any building or institution named after you, which would you choose? Why?

Collections of fun questions are available in books like *The Book of Questions* (Workman Publishing, 1987) and *IF: Questions for the Game of Life* (Villard, 1995), or in game form in a product called *Table Topics Conversation Cards.*

I believe that people are longing for connection—in the workplace and in their lives generally. The exercises that are part of this step involve more than just getting to know your coachee so that you can create meaningful goals and promote enhanced performance from him. They also involve making a deeper connection with another person—something we all want to do and something that makes the workplace warmer and more human. Be creative and curious. Discovery is one of the most fun parts of coaching and of being human.

Applying the Learning

◆ Make it a point to find out all you can this week about a new coachee, an existing coachee, or one of your employees, using a variety of tools from this step—personality typing, input from others, observations, values identification, skills and accomplishments assessments, or fun questions. Put the information you learn in a very visible spot in his coachee/employee folder so that you can refer to it often during future coaching sessions.

◆ What are your spouse's/partner's values? Your direct reports' values? Your own? Your coachee's? Are they being honored now?

◆ Do you know your own strengths, weaknesses, opportunities, and threats? Perhaps you want to give others a 360-degree feedback instrument to complete on your behalf.

◆ Practice giving at least two pieces of feedback that are solicited, immediate, specific, balanced, achievable, and genuine. Try to share the impact of the coachee's observed behavior as well as a suggestion, where applicable. Make sure you give the recipient time to respond.

◆ This week, use five of the questions found in this step with someone in your organization. (There are plenty in exam-

> POINTER
>
> A moment's insight is sometimes worth a life's experience.
> – Oliver Wendell Holmes, Sr., physician and writer

ples 4.4 and 4.5, as well as in the section "Discovery Forms and Fun Questions.") Notice how knowing the answers to these questions affects your relationship with that person going forward.

NOTES

_____

_____

_____

_____

_____

_____

_____

_____

_____

_____

_____

_____

_____

_____

_____

_____

_____

_____

_____

_____

Agree on What You Want to Accomplish

STEP **5**

I used to have a *New Yorker* cartoon in my office that showed a man standing beside a poster of a very simple three-step flowchart. The arrow at the top of the chart read, "Start," the box at the bottom read, "End," and the middle arrow read, "Something wonderful happens here." The caption at the bottom of the cartoon was the voice of someone in this man's audience asking, "Can you be a little more specific about that middle step?"

Coaching is something wonderful, but what's going to come of it will need to be defined. Otherwise, your sessions will be as ambiguous and confusing as the middle step in my cartoon.

You and your coachee will need to agree about what she wants to be coached on (focus) and what outcomes she is seeking (goals). Determining the focus for coaching is like coming up with the title for a workshop. For example, a training workshop in which all the exercises will address getting a better handle on one's daily, weekly, and monthly schedules might be titled "Time Management Workshop." In the same way, time management would be the focus of a coaching program that addresses the coachee's ability to plan her schedules more effectively. When you have a title for your training workshop, you devise an activities agenda that serves the stated topic. Those activities are analogous to the goals in a coaching program—the individual steps a coachee takes to achieve the focus.

Where Should We Focus the Coaching?

Many people in the workplace want some of this wonderful thing called coaching, but they don't know what they want coaching to focus on. For example, people being groomed for positions of greater responsibility might have been told they'd benefit from having a coach, but they don't know quite where to begin.

Just saying "We're going to work together as coach and coachee" isn't really enough. Among other things, you'll need to know whether you're working together on career path coaching, money management coaching, leadership coaching, or some other type of coaching.

Example 5.1 is one way for coach and coachee to identify possible coaching topics. The ratings your coachee assigns to her current levels of satisfaction in each area are good tools for determining what you'll focus on. You can coach her in the areas she scored lowest if you want to raise her competency in (and, therefore, her satisfaction with) those skill areas; or you may agree to concentrate on the topics that give her the greatest satisfaction if you want to capitalize on her strengths. You also might want to find out how she arrived at the numbers she assigned. Which of these areas does she feel are most critical in her position? And how much time is she currently allocating to those that are more—or less—critical? Obviously, there are lots of ways to go with the information you'll get from this activity.

Some of the questions you asked in Step 4—What changes do you want to make? What would you be doing if time and resources were plentiful?—are also helpful in defining how your time together

EXAMPLE 5.1

Topics for Coaching

Coachee instructions: The left-hand column contains a list of topics you may want to focus on in coaching. The bottom of the form asks for any other topics you may want to add. In the right-hand column, circle the appropriate number to indicate your present level of satisfaction with each item. 1 = not at all satisfied; 10 = completely satisfied.

Topic	Level of Satisfaction
Quality of my work product	1 2 3 4 5 6 7 8 9 10
My efficiency	1 2 3 4 5 6 7 8 9 10
Relationship with my boss	1 2 3 4 5 6 7 8 9 10
Relationship with my team	1 2 3 4 5 6 7 8 9 10
My leadership abilities	1 2 3 4 5 6 7 8 9 10
My creativity	1 2 3 4 5 6 7 8 9 10
My visibility in the organization	1 2 3 4 5 6 7 8 9 10
My time management	1 2 3 4 5 6 7 8 9 10
My work/life balance	1 2 3 4 5 6 7 8 9 10
My career path	1 2 3 4 5 6 7 8 9 10
	1 2 3 4 5 6 7 8 9 10
	1 2 3 4 5 6 7 8 9 10
	1 2 3 4 5 6 7 8 9 10
	1 2 3 4 5 6 7 8 9 10
	1 2 3 4 5 6 7 8 9 10
	1 2 3 4 5 6 7 8 9 10

Source: Adapted from the work of Caryn Siegel, CJS Consulting, and used with permission.

will be spent. They're a good place to start as you agree on a focus for coaching.

Goal Setting

Now that you and your coachee have a focus, what does addressing that focus look like? Where does your coachee want to be in relation to this focus? This ideal state will become her goal. Those goals form your itinerary for coaching. They are the reference points that you will keep coming back to and checking on. Goals are going to be where there is definite proof that the coachee is moving somewhere, and goals are the finish line that the coachee is striving to reach.

I'm not suggesting that the goals you and your coachee set will remain static during your work together. It's often true that goals need to be adjusted as you go. When goals change, it's a positive reminder that they are living things. When a coachee wants to change a goal, it says that she's been thinking about it in a meaningful way rather than just hanging it on her wall as background art.

When it comes time for goal setting, use whatever format works for you and your coachee. The format you choose to establish will depend on many factors, including whether your coachee is more detail oriented or more of a big-picture person, whether she responds well to written road maps or to her instincts, or whether the goals will be shared with others.

Many of you will use SMART goals. This type of goal has been popular for some time. The acronym SMART reminds you that your goals should be **S**pecific, **M**easurable, **A**chievable, **R**ealistic, and **T**imely. (Don't be alarmed if your understanding of SMART goals differs slightly from the terms I've used here. SMART goals have been used extensively and some people have substituted similar terms to define them.)

I use what I call "3-T" goals. They're like SMART goals, but I've taken a couple of SMART aspects out and added one aspect that I feel is lacking in SMART goals—a tie-in to something that makes you want to achieve the goal in the first place. When people sit down to write their goals, something usually motivates them to do so. But written goals generally don't include that primary motivation. That's too bad because remembering why the goal is important to them can reenergize coachees when their efforts to reach their goals have failed and they're feeling discouraged or overwhelmed. I like to include right there in the written goal the hook that will keep the coachee moving toward her goal on those days when she hardly can recall why the goal was important. 3-T goals are **T**angible, **T**ime bound, and **T**ied to something that matters to you. The arrows in figure 5.1 show how SMART goals map to 3-T goals.

Here are some examples of 3-T goals:

◆ Two months from now *[time bound],* I'll have a system to follow up on calls and letters, I'll be on time, get all tasks accomplished, and have realistic goals for new projects *[tangible].* I choose to do all of this in the service of my value of being there for others *[tied to something that matters].*

◆ To deepen my relationship with Rodney and to help him become more fulfilled and productive in his job *[tied to something that matters],* by next Friday *[time bound],* I will ask him to work with me as my coachee *[tangible].*

FIGURE 5.1

SMART Goals and 3-T Goals

SMART	3-T
Specific	Tangible—*Well defined, detailed, visual (so that you can recognize when this goal has been reached)*
Measurable	
Achievable	Time bound—*Clear about the date by which it will be achieved*
Realistic	
Timely	Tied to something that matters to you—*Explicit about why this goal is important; what values the coachee honors in doing this*

Let's talk about "tangible" for a moment. Something that's tangible can be felt or observed; something obvious. Some goals are more easily made tangible than are others. One of the main determinants of how tangible you can make your goals is based on the distinction between what the coachee wants to accomplish and who she wants to become. Some things she wants are certain outward accomplishments—a transfer to a new position in the organization, to finish a report or presentation, to receive a raise. These goals are often shorter-term outcomes and are more easily observable. Others are more internal and intangible, like becoming more trusting, more approachable, more confident, or less of a micromanager. These goals have more to do with who the coachee is in the workplace, and they usually require more time and deeper exploration to realize. However, these goals are often the ones that are going to have the greatest positive impact on the individual and the organization.

It's easy for some of the "doing" tasks in one's life to be described in concrete terms (I will get to work 20 minutes earlier each day, I will speak up three times in every meeting); it's harder to do so with some of the "being" tasks. But you can make measurable something like being more trusting. For instance, I ask my clients to give me a number between 1 and 10 that describes how trusting they are and a number that describes how trusting they want to become. Our resulting goal sounds something like this: "Over the next six months, I want to come to trust my employees at a level of 8. That will make my relationships with them easier and more fun and give me back some of the time I now spend checking up on them."

To further highlight this distinction between doing and being, let's take an item from that coaching topics list (example 5.1), visibility in the organization. A "doing" outcome to increase your coachee's visibility might be publishing an article in the company newsletter or heading an important project team; a "being" outcome might be growing more comfortable stating her accomplishments or being in the limelight.

Usually your coachee can achieve "being" tasks without "doing" anything (that is, she might become more comfortable in the limelight, even if she hasn't published an article or addressed a group of colleagues); but it's hard to do anything when you're not ready or able to "be" a particular way (for example, it's more difficult to head up a project team when you're uncomfortable being visible). Another example: I might become more organized without creating a new scheduling system, but I doubt that I can create a scheduling system when I'm completely disorganized or feeling out of control of my time.

Another aspect of tangible goals is that they can be measured easily. When working with measurable goals, remember that you'll want to collect baseline data right at the start of the coaching relationship. You'll use this data later to track your coachee's advancement. This data collection can be as simple as a verbal review of how confident, nervous, energetic, powerful, happy, or engaged your coachee feels today, on a scale of 1 to 10. Of course, baseline data can be more rigorous as well. Some things one might track to measure a coachee's progress over time include

- turnover rate among coachee's direct reports
- employee attendance patterns
- morale scores on a survey
- number of awards received by the coachee
- number of emails sent each day
- number of meetings on calendar each day
- number of presentations given
- performance review scores of coachee or coachee's direct reports.

When you have these baseline measurements, you can return to them at intervals throughout your coaching, looking for trends over time as well as for evidence of progress.

And now a few words about tying goals to something meaningful. You might notice in the examples I provided that, when talking about the tie-in, these goals usually contain the word "my"—my value of being there for others, my relationship with Rodney. That's because this component has to address what's meaningful to the coachee, the person creating the goals.

Therefore, statements like the following do not count as ties to something meaningful: "because I was told to," "because it's part of my job," or "to keep my job." These statements may be true, but they're "shoulds," and they aren't particularly inspiring. If these are the reasons that your coachee is sharing with you, probe more deeply: Why do you want to do it just because you were told to? Why do you want to keep your job? The answers to those questions are the significant facts that compel your coachee to do something—"it gives me pleasure to check things off my list," "I feel complete when I'm doing what people expect of me," or "my paycheck lets me live the life I enjoy." Similarly, "because my employees will benefit greatly from it" doesn't fly here. That's why the goal is meaningful to your coachee's employees, not why it's meaningful to her. Maybe that translates into something like "because I feel satisfied and happy when I help others" or "because when my employees are benefiting, they're more positive and my work environment improves." In setting goals, as in coaching as a whole, the focus is on the coachee and her desires and needs.

I had a powerful illustration of the importance of tying action to what's personally meaningful in a meeting of my boss (the HR director for Redwood City), the city manager, and me. We'd gotten together to talk about succession planning citywide. My boss and I really needed our boss (the city manager) to champion succession planning. But he told us honestly that although this was something he knew we should *(there's that awful word again!)* be doing, it wasn't something he was excited about. My boss expertly tied succession planning to what was the city manager's passion (community building), pointing out that if key positions became vacant, community building would be stalled and the community would become frustrated with the lack of staff responsiveness. This connection was all it took for the city manager to realize how important succession planning was to him and to the initiatives he held dear to his heart. From that point forward, he wholeheartedly supported it.

Again, you don't have to use 3-T or SMART goals, but you will want something that puts into place a vision toward which your coachee can strive.

Action Planning

When you and your coachee have pictured where she is going, she'll need to start thinking about how she's going to get there. Again, how this is recorded or thought about will vary, depending on the coachee. Some people prefer a more formal and detailed plan, as in example 5.2. Others want a visual reminder like the fishbone action plan in example 5.3. Still others prefer a more casual, short-term planning device, as you'll find in example 5.4.

Example 5.2 is a form I've used with clients in more formal organizations to clarify goals and articulate why the goals were chosen. The third, fourth, and fifth columns outline the actions, resources, and time needed to achieve these goals.

Example 5.3 will appeal to more visual and less formal coachees. This is the classic fishbone exercise (it's called a fishbone because that's what the arrow with each of its propelling forces and barriers looks like). When the coachee has filled in the fishbone, we brainstorm how to get past the obstacles she's listed there.

For coachees who prefer not to create an action plan around their goals, but to think about what needs to be done as they move along, send a questionnaire (like example 5.4) prior to each coaching session. On this report, the coachee can recap progress made since the last session and prepare for immediate next steps. The answers on this report also serve as an agenda of sorts for the upcoming coaching session. Some of my clients send me their responses in advance, some just bring them to the session for us to refer to as needed.

If your coachee is having trouble thinking of "propelling forces" (as used in example 5.3), using other terminology might help. To prompt a coachee to identify her propelling forces, you might ask her what her assets are. These assets may be personal qualities or characteristics (such as a positive outlook or an ability to hire good people) or organizational attributes (such as strong senior leadership, community support, or cash in reserve). When you've brainstormed assets, you're in a position to determine how to build on them to achieve the coachee's goal.

EXAMPLE 5.2

Individual Development Plan

Coachee instructions: Use the column on the far left to list the goals that are most important for you to achieve. Then, for each goal, answer the questions in the other four columns.

Most important goals to achieve right now	What criteria were used to select this as a goal?	What steps need to be taken to accomplish this goal?	What help or support do you need from your coach? From others?	What is your timeframe for achieving this goal?

Source: Full Experience Coaching.

EXAMPLE 5.3

Fishbone Action Planning

Coachee instructions: Write a goal inside the arrow. On the slanted line above the arrow, list all the forces that are propelling you toward achieving this goal. On the slanted lines below the arrow, list forces that are barring your ability to achieve the goal. After brainstorming with your coach, list five actions you can take to overcome the barriers.

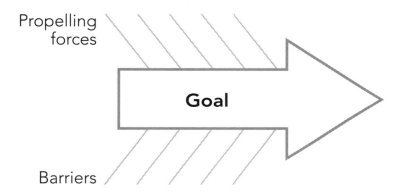

Propelling forces

Goal

Barriers

STEP 5

What five things can I do to overcome the barriers?

1.

2.

3.

4.

5.

EXAMPLE 5.4

Weekly Progress Check

Coachee instructions: For a goal that you are working on, use the questions below to monitor your progress and to establish intentions for continuing to move ahead.

My goal:	
How am I generally feeling about reaching this goal right now?	
What two actions did I take this week to lead me closer to my goal?	
What stood in the way of my forward movement this week? What do I want to do about these obstacles?	
What aspect of this goal do I want to discuss in my upcoming coaching session?	
What are my intentions around this goal for the coming week(s)?	

Source: Full Experience Coaching.

Another word to replace propelling forces is "motivators." What are those things that will move your coachee to action in a given situation? Does she have an internal competitiveness or desire to succeed? Does she seek positions of more responsibility? Example 5.5 is a great tool for coaches and managers alike. It helps define more

EXAMPLE 5.5

What Motivates You?

Coachee instructions: Read the scenario. Then rank each of the 12 potential rewards. To the right of each reward, put a number from 1 to 12, with 1 being the most appealing reward and 12 being the least appealing.

The scenario: *You have just managed a challenging project—one that some people thought was set up to fail. You completed it on time and on budget, and your team still likes you. Your boss hands you the following list of possible rewards for a job well done and asks you to rate them.*

Reward	Number
No reward—I get satisfaction from successfully completing assigned tasks like this one	
Praise from my boss and team members	
Some time off after working so hard on this project	
Financial compensation for coming in under budget	
My boss publicly announcing the results so that my visibility in the organization increases	
Being given other challenging assignments like this one now that I've shown my stuff	
More autonomy and control on future projects; earning more trust in my abilities from my boss	
A note placed in my personnel file	
This success counting toward a possible promotion	
A gift card to my favorite store or activity	
A budget to take the project team out to celebrate our accomplishment	
I've got a better idea: [write your own reward]	

Source: Full Experience Coaching.

narrowly the types of recognition your coachees/employees most appreciate. These motivators can become the propelling forces that help them achieve their goals. Before giving this questionnaire to a coachee, you may want to rework it a bit—possibly changing the scenario provided to one that more closely matches the coachee's specific goals.

Don't assume that, as someone's coach or manager, you already know how she's going to respond to this questionnaire. A study back in the 1990s in which employees and their bosses were each asked to rate the factors that would motivate the employees showed a huge discrepancy in perceived priorities on this subject. Managers, asked to guess which factors on a list were most motivating to their employees, ranked good wages, job security, and promotion opportunities as first, second, and third, respectively. Their employees ranked those factors fifth, fourth, and seventh. The employees' top three? Appreciation, feeling "in" on things, and an understanding attitude. What results might this disconnection between managers and employees have had?

Accountability

You would think that tying coachees' goals to what matters to them would ensure that coachees would follow through on the goals they've set. Not so. Have you ever had an employee who agreed to do things you requested of her, or who took on tasks that she knew would be great for her professionally, only to have her repeatedly neglect to follow through on what she'd committed to do? I've witnessed situations like these countless times. Coaching can't be one of those times. Accountability begins in this step and is a constant throughout coaching.

The dictionary definition of accountability is "being subject to giving a statement explaining one's conduct, or a statement or exposition of reasons, causes, grounds or motives for action; being answerable." Ask your coachee how she would like to be answerable to you. Ask for permission to follow up using questions like thes: How will I know you did that? By when will you do that? or How did that assignment work for you? Ask your coachee what she wants you to say or do when she doesn't do what she's said she will do.

It's often true, too, that employees (or coachees) who don't do well at follow-through have supervisors (or coaches) who also don't do well at follow-through. Accountability is about following through, and follow-through is sorely lacking in our society. How are you with follow-through? Do you return calls and emails within 24–48 hours? Do you send the things you say you're going to send to people within the promised timeframe? When was the last time you wrote a thank-you note? Would people say they can count on you to complete the tasks that you've agreed to perform, especially when it affects their ability to do their work? Do you conduct de-briefing meetings after events and projects? Before you are a coach, you are an employee, perhaps a manager, and a role model to your employees and coachees. Just showing that you're a person who is accountable is significant.

This point in the coaching relationship is also the time to re-mind the coachee that the success of coaching relies on her—that what she gets out of it is in direct proportion to what she puts in to it. Find out whether she is committed to the process of coaching. What does that commitment mean to her? What does it look like?

Accountability will come up again in Step 8 when you're think-ing about how to realign with your coachee when things aren't go-ing so well and, specifically, when your coachee isn't following through with her assignments. Establishing your expectations of ac-countability now will serve you well in those later discussions.

Time is precious, and it's important that you and your coachee know what will make the time you spend together worthwhile. How are you defining success? And how are you holding her accountable for achieving that success? Simply writing 3-T goals—with tangible and time-bound outcomes that are tied to something meaningful to the coachee—can build accountability in and of itself. Coaching can produce wonderful results if you have planned for them. Otherwise, the potential results can be missed, overwhelmed, or set aside.

Remember to hold a "soft focus" for the coachee's goals (an intention or awareness of where you want to be that you're willing to give up if goals change). When goals change, it's a sign of growth and consideration. Goals and plans are important, but coaching is dynamic and responsive.

Applying the Learning

- ◆ What does your coachee want the coaching to focus on? Have you named the focal topic of your coaching? If not, pull out example 5.1 to help narrow it down.
- ◆ Establish a 3-T or SMART goal with your coachee or for yourself. Is it tangible, time-bound, and tied to something meaningful? Is it related to the focal topic?
- ◆ What will propel your coachee toward her goals? What obstacles might she face?
- ◆ What motivates your coachee? Use example 5.5 to rank those things that will help your coachee remain active in pursuing her goals.
- ◆ Is your coachee aware of how you will hold her accountable? For what are you accountable in the coaching relationship?

STEP **5**

STEP
5

Use the Power of Possibility

OVERVIEW

Three coaching skills: championing, acknowledging, and visualizing

How to use questions most effectively

Details of coach listening

In my coaching practice, I not only enjoy the privilege of having people share with me their secret (or not-so-secret) dreams; I also have the privilege of helping them see that they can turn these dreams into reality. Granted, this transformation doesn't always happen, but at every moment of coaching I hold the strong belief that my coachee's dreams, and even more, are possible.

STEP **6**

This step in the coaching process is the one where you help others dream and plan bigger than they think they can. And why do you do this? Certainly it's not so they can fall flat on their faces. You do it so they can realize their brilliance and their possibilities.

Because of their strengths, people can accomplish far more than they think they can. Coaches let them know that by using the skill of *championing*. Showing individuals their own brilliance is accomplished by *acknowledging* who they are—recognizing the wonderful traits that they have and that they are displaying. Sometimes coachees believe in themselves but don't know how to make their dreams materialize. That's where the skill of *visualizing* comes into play.

The Skill of Championing

A coach must truly believe in his or her coachee. When the coachee says, "I can't give a presentation to the senior management team," the coach says, "You can." When the coachee says, "I want to start a new business 10 years or so down the road," the coach says, "How about next year?"

I remember a fellow participant in my very first coaching class saying that this approach seemed very irresponsible. How can a coach encourage someone to do something that he might not be ready or able to do? My course leaders said something then that has stuck with me: People have enough naysayers in their lives—kind people who simply don't want them to "get their hopes up," to get hurt or disappointed, to fail. And coaches can't just add their voices to that din.

Coaches are not afraid of people failing or getting their hopes dashed. They generally believe that people are capable, powerful, and terrific. They know that their coachees are strong enough to handle hardships in pursuit of their goals. And they know that if not pushed to their highest levels of magnificence, their coachees are robbing the world of their greatness. People do not need another protector; they need someone who will inspire them and expand their possibilities.

Think of a sports coach. Do you think that her players would get anywhere if she was afraid her players would fall down, be injured, or lose a game? In fact, a coach feels her coachee has to experience these circumstances to learn and improve.

Your coachee knows his own limits only too well. If you ask him to do something he's not comfortable with, your relationship should be strong enough for him to say "no." But who knows? He may counter with an offer greater than his original thought. Here's how that might sound:

> **Coachee:** I need to talk to that employee about her continued lateness, but I just keep getting too busy and it falls off the radar...

Coach: What if you cut out everything you said after "but"? What if we ended our session now—early—and you went out there and got her and spent our remaining 20 minutes having that conversation?

Coachee: Now? But I'm not ready. I really want to have all my facts straight—like how often she's been late—before we talk.

Coach: You can say "yes" or "no," or you can make a counteroffer. Are you saying "no"?

Coachee: I guess I am saying "no" to that. But, OK, how about this as a counteroffer? What if we end early and I spend the 20 minutes gathering the data I need?

Coach: Great. What if you do that, and if you also pick up the phone and schedule a meeting with her for the end of this week?

Coachee: I could do that . . . and then I'd have a real impetus to finish my fact-finding today!

Here are a few ways to stretch your championing muscles. Try the following actions with your coachee (if you don't have one yet, enlist a friend, family member, or colleague who wants to live his or her biggest dreams).

◆ **"What's bigger"?** Ask your coachee, "What's your dream?" Let him tell you all about it. Ask "What's even bigger than that?" Let him answer, and then ask again, "What's bigger than that?" Ask this four or five times—no kidding. Then ask, "What's possible for you to do right now to move toward this dream? Here's how the conversation might sound:

> **Coach:** What's your dream?
>
> **Coachee:** I want to open a senior citizen center.
>
> **Coach:** Great. Tell me more about it. What's going on at your senior center?
>
> **Coachee:** It's a place where seniors come and remain active in the things they've always loved. If they loved to cook, they cook the meals. If they enjoyed playing or listening to music, they can do that with local musi-

cians who drop in. And if they're near the end of their lives, there's a hospice wing with counselors to make their final days peaceful.

Coach: That's a beautiful vision. And I'm curious, what's bigger than that dream?

Coachee: What do you mean?

Coach: I mean what could your dream hold that's even bigger than that picture you just gave me?

Coachee: Well, I guess it could also have an organic garden tended by seniors and community volunteers. It could make money when the seniors sell the produce in their own store. It could be a local pet-sitting service. The elderly would have the company of the pets and the pet owners would have a reasonably priced option.

Coach: OK. What's even bigger?

Coachee: Hmmm. It could be featured on the news and be a model for other centers across the nation.

Coach: And what's bigger?

Coachee: I guess I could be famous for reforming senior care options.

Coach: So what do you want to do right now in your quest to become famous for reforming senior care?

Coachee: I guess I need to start getting famous by speaking about senior care at public events. . . .

◆ **"You can do that."** The next time someone tells you his big idea, notice how you're naturally inclined to respond. Do you start in with the challenges he'll face, the things you want him to consider, or the reasons it's not a good time? Don't judge your response—just notice it. The time after that, don't just notice where you tend to go, but also take yourself to the "you can do that" frame of mind. Listen and give an unqualified, "Yes," and see what's possible from that place. Where does the conversation go when you're approaching it from a positive frame of mind?

◆ **Where am I holding back?** List the names of your coachees and employees and the important people in your life. For each person, consider where you might be protecting him or holding him back. When are you thinking small about what he's capable of doing or becoming?

A coach afraid to champion her coachee, afraid to support him wholeheartedly in whatever he's doing (provided it's safe and legal) is thinking too egocentrically about herself. It's not as if the coachee will do whatever the coach says. But that moment when the coachee has someone believing in him may be just enough time for new doors to open and something he never thought possible to come through those doors.

One tricky part of championing is taking it too far and making it into an agenda. I've done this—I've really made it "wrong" for a client to do anything other than go for his biggest possible dream. What I learned that the coach needs to remember is that this dream must remain the coachee's dream for himself. If, for whatever reason, the coachee is choosing to downsize or not to follow his dream, that's got to be OK. Championing a coachee's dream simply lets him know that if he wants it, he can achieve it.

The Skill of Acknowledging

One of the reasons people can't see themselves doing great things is that they don't see their own greatness. The world is pretty good at helping people see their weaknesses or limitations, but slow to help them know their strengths and magnificence. Even those enlightened ones who know that they're damned good may have a hard time promoting themselves because they've been taught that bragging is bad and they have no healthy ways to toot their own horns.

A coach can help her coachee accomplish great things by acknowledging what she sees in the coachee. It's like holding a mirror in front of a person and helping him see in himself what you see in him. The key in that phrase is *"in* him." Acknowledging goes be-

yond simply recognizing people's accomplishments or their successes; it reveals what you see at their core—perhaps a good person, a
smart person, a thoughtful person, or a powerful person.

You might need some practice to get comfortable with this skill
of acknowledging, of truly knowing your coachee. Here are some
ways to do that:

- Use worksheet 6.1 to acknowledge several aspects of people
  you know well—for example, your employees. Recall and
  make note of what they've accomplished. List their essen-
  tial characteristics. Then go deeper to consider who they
  are at the core of their beings. Write a descriptive phrase/
  metaphor that reveals that core. You might even go so far
  as to share some of this with the people you've included.

- When you meet someone for the first time, listen as he
  tells you about himself. Stay aware of what personal
  strengths he's revealing by what he chooses to tell you and
  how he tells it, by his nonverbal communication, and by
  the way he stands or sits. Challenge yourself to slip some
  sort of acknowledgment into the conversation—for example, "I know you'll figure that issue out because I can see
  you're wise and self-aware," or "Your employees really are
  lucky to have you as their boss—I can see you're fair and
  open," or "You're clearly a caring parent."

- Try an acknowledgment in every conversation this week.
  This is similar to the last exercise, but instead of just trying out acknowledgments in situations with strangers, see
  what happens when you intentionally do it with each person you speak with.

People get noticed for their awards, speeches, and promotions,
for their tangible successes. How much more would they be capable
of if we also noticed them just for being who they are? How much
more could they accomplish if they saw themselves in the positive
light in which you see them?

WORKSHEET 6.1

What They Do and Who They Are

Instructions: List your coachees/employees. Then consider what they've accomplished and what characteristics they possess. Finally, write an analogy to describe who each one is at her or his core. An example is provided.

Person	Accomplishments	Characteristics	Analogy to describe her/his core
Jane Smith	Led terrific team retreat, has loyal reports (lowest turnover rate in organization), successful client project	Honest, hard worker, warm, inspiring, fun	Jane is like the sun shining on a field of flowers. She lights up her people and produces beautiful results.

The Skill of Visualizing

There are two things that make the possibility of doing what you want to do more likely to happen. One is publicly stating your intention or goal aloud. The other is painting a really vivid picture of your vision. This is partly so that you can recognize it when it actually happens. I've seen some coachees let the opportunity they'd long been waiting for slip right past them because they were caught up in whatever it was they were already doing and didn't realize how this seeming sidetrack was really what they'd been talking and thinking about for months.

Painting a vivid picture of the vision also is useful when your coachee shares it with others in his life. Then he has not merely one person working to make his dream happen, but his whole support system looking out for him as well. Finally, having a clear picture helps propel the coachee forward on days when his dream seems way out of reach.

POINTER

Many of my clients have created **vision boards** since they were popularized in the bestselling DVD, *The Secret*. A vision board is a collage or other visual representation of what you want at a given time. The idea is that keeping in front of you an image of what you want to have or to do in your life will keep you connected to your dream, stimulate you to action, and help you recognize it when it manifests itself. It's not enough simply to make a vision board, sit back, and wait for everything on it to materialize, but it is a tool that's meaningful and helpful to some people.

It's very simple to make a vision board, even if you don't consider yourself artistic or creative. Cut out pictures, scribble words, or sketch images of where you want to live, what you want to do, how you want to look, what you want to acquire, and so forth. Paste all of these images and words together on a large poster or gather them into whatever format you prefer. Post your vision board in a prominent place, and see how it moves you toward your goals and dreams.

When a coachee tells you his goal—whether for a project, a team, a career change, or whatever—probe deeply to make it as tangible as you can. Who's around when he reaches this goal? What does he hear, see, taste, smell at that point? What's the predominant color or setting? When he pictures it clearly, what's happening and what's going to happen after that?

For a coachee who likes visual reminders of what he's moving toward, ask him to find pictures of what he's described to you and to post them around his office. A simple visual cue sometimes is all it takes to keep a person tuned in to his vision. That's why it helps to ask about the sensory details. For example, if his vision of a dream home has a lot of yellow in it, carrying around a yellow file folder will help him stay in touch with that vision every day.

Aligning Dreams with Values

Whether we're faced with a task we really want to do—or one we'd really like to avoid—it's important to know why we're doing it. We often do things without questioning or because we "should." We do things to reach a particular outcome without considering the other potential outcomes we'll encounter. We may continue working toward a dream without realizing it isn't still the one we want.

What's going to hold a coachee to his dreams is how closely his actions and dreams fit with what's important to him. You already learned your coachee's values in your earlier work with him. How does his dream tie in with those values?

For example, one of my clients dreamed of starting her own website and eventually publishing a book comprising the columns she'd included on her blog. When she tried to make time to write her columns, however, she grew discouraged. She started questioning all parts of her dream. "Who am I kidding?" she said. "It's impossible to get a book deal. I'll never get enough done to fill a book. This could take me another 10 years." What did compel her to write some columns for the blog was realizing that each column she wrote helped her honor her values of connecting with others and repairing the world.

Transformative Power of Questions

What can break people out of a rut? What can jump-start their thinking about possibilities? What's the ultimate coaching tool for helping coachees turn their dreams into reality? Questions. The power of questions to get people thinking deeply and creatively is truly amazing.

The Coaches Training Institute explains that questions "open a door to discovery by asking rather than telling." Questions get past people's defenses and prompt them to devise answers that work for them.

Peter Ingram was the public works director when I was employee development manager for Redwood City, CA. One afternoon, he sat down with one of his division's supervisors to talk about staffing in his division. The meeting wasn't going especially well. There was lots of blaming and frustration on the part of the supervisor who wasn't certain that existing staff members had the capacity or passion to create success. He also was annoyed with the amount of time he had to spend on operational tasks and issues. After a moment's thought, Ingram popped in a powerful question that changed the future of the department: Where are your passions? The supervisor visibly relaxed and began to talk about water conservation and how much he really wanted to take that program to a whole new level. Ingram reports, "I was so clear on what he felt he could do if given the chance that we began to explore the ultimate organizational change we made—to create a new water conservation program for the city."

Not all questions have that much power. The kinds of questions that do have it are curious, open-ended, bold, and often naïve. They're the questions that are hanging out in the room but no one's asking; the questions the coachee is forgetting to ask himself.

They're the questions that really want to get at the heart of the matter, or at the heart of the person being asked.

Where do you find the questions? Everywhere (or you can use the question generator in tool 6.1). Here are some suggestions:

◆ **Build off what the coachee says,** as in this example:

> *Coach:* What do you want to talk about today?

> *Coachee:* I don't know. I feel confused.

TOOL 6.1

Question Generator

Instructions: Pick one word or phrase from columns 1, 2, and 3 to create more than 125 questions.

Column 1	Column 2	Column 3
What's	happening	
	possible	
	working	
	needed	
	your wish	
	your role	for you?
	the sticking place	right now?
	not being said	from this perspective?
	your choice	when you get/do that?
	important	in the big picture?
	fun	for/in that meeting/
	next	interaction?
		for/in your team?
Who	is responsible	as a leader?
	do you need to be	in five years?
How	will you do/get that	
	will this work	
	do you feel	
	can you be *[insert adjective here]*	

Coach: What's the confusion about?

Coachee: I don't know how I feel about the new employee.

Coach: It sounds like you do know, but aren't saying it. How do you feel about him?

Coachee: Well, he's not motivated, and I'm not sure I can motivate him.

Coach: How might you motivate him?

Coachee: I tried the same things that have worked with other employees, but they didn't work with him. I'm not sure what to do next.

Coach: So, what *might* you try next?

◆ **Ask the dumb questions,** the ones that only a naïve person would ask. These are the questions that you'd often think to preface with "Pardon my stupidity, but. . . ." These are questions like, Why do you think that? Why do you have to? Who told you that you had to? Is *[fill in]* true? and Isn't *[fill in]* also true?

◆ **Read up.** In the "self-help" section of your library or local bookstore, you'll find titles loaded with questions. Here are some examples: Byron Katie's *Loving What Is: Four Questions That Can Change Your Life* (Harmony, 2002); Marilee G. Adams' *Change Your Questions, Change Your Life: 7 Powerful Tools for Life and Work* (Berrett-Koehler, 2004); and Michael J. Marquardt's *Leading with Questions: How Leaders Find the Right Solutions by Knowing What to Ask* (Jossey-Bass, 2005). Not only are these books full of tried and truly powerful questions, but they're also fascinating reading.

◆ **Ask questions from your gut.** Many questions live in your gut but you've been taught to hold them there, not to be nosy or inappropriate. Be curious. If you have a question burning inside you, blurt it out.

◆ **Ask your coachee for questions.** The coachee drives the coaching process, so ask him, "What's the question you need to ask yourself about this situation?" My clients come up with brilliant questions for themselves all the time.

At each of the 10 steps in the coaching process, there are questions it's appropriate and helpful to ask. Tool 6.2 presents a list of them, arranged by step. These aren't the only questions that work at each step—they aren't even necessarily the best questions. But they are questions that will help you achieve what's meant to be achieved at each step. As you add your own favorites to the list, keep it in front of you as a tickler when you work with your first few coachees.

Questions We're Not Asking

These are the types of questions we avoid in coaching:

◆ **"Why" questions.** Coaching has as its focus the present moment and how the coachee can get from the present moment to the desired future. This is not the place for analyzing how a person got into his present circumstance or situation. We don't ask, Why are you in this predicament? or Why do you think you feel that way? Leave it to therapists to determine why someone believes as he does or what happened in his past to create the situation he's in now. Why questions (Why did you do that? Why didn't you do this?) also can put coachees on the defensive.

◆ **"Why don't you . . . " questions.** Coaches want coachees to come up with solutions themselves. Asking, Why don't you call that person today? or Why don't you look for a new job? implies that the coach has the correct answer and, indeed, will judge the coachee if he chooses another approach. Also, because a "why don't you. . . ?" question is phrased in the negative, people tend to give a negative answer (for example, Why don't you make that call? Because I don't want to!). If instead you ask, What would you do to remedy this situation? people are guided to think positively.

◆ **Questions about details.** This step is about greatness. Greatness doesn't lie in the stories coachees tell, it lies in what they're capable of doing or becoming. You can do a

TOOL 6.2

Questions to Ask at Each of the 10 Steps

Step	Questions
Step 1: Prepare Yourself for the Coaching Role	*Ask yourself:* • What's my definition of coaching? • What do I need to have in place to be a good coach? • What do I want from coaching? • What excites me about coaching?
Step 2: Remove Personal Obstacles	*Ask yourself:* • What gremlins are present for me around coaching? • What do I want to do with them? • At what other time have I overcome obstacles to do what I wanted to do?
Step 3: Create Your Coaching Relationship(s)	*Ask your coachee:* • What expectations do you have of yourself or me, your coach? • What kind of meeting schedule would work for you? • Where would you like to meet? • To what amount of time shall we commit?

- What kinds of information would you be open to sharing (for example, personnel file, 360-degree evaluations, and the like)?
- How will we know if this relationship is working?
- How will we know when it's time to stop?
- What's the best way to deal with you when you're resistant to coaching?

Step 4: Find Out About Your Coachee

Ask your coachee:

- What's your favorite childhood memory?
- What is your idea of fun?
- Who is someone who inspires you, and why?
- Will you describe a perfect day?
- What is one of your greatest accomplishments, and why?
- What is your favorite book/movie/song? What memories are associated with it?
- Which assignments or role in the past provided you with the greatest challenge? The least? Why?
- What makes you unique?
- What lessons have you learned from your successes or failures?
- What part of your education or work experience has been the most valuable to you over the years?

continued on next page

STEP
6

Tool 6.2, continued

Step	Questions
Step 5: Agree on What You Want to Accomplish	*Ask your coachee:* ◆ What is it to be a leader/boss? ◆ How does this goal fit in with your plans/way of life/values? ◆ Why are you here? ◆ What in your life do you want to change? ◆ What obstacles are in your way? ◆ What can you do now and in the long term to get you there? ◆ What tools/resources do you require? ◆ How will you know you've changed? ◆ What does success look like for this goal? ◆ By when will you achieve it? ◆ Why is this goal important to you?
Step 6: Use the Power of Possibility	*Ask your coachee:* ◆ What excites you? ◆ What's next? ◆ What do you want? ◆ What's your dream? ◆ What's bigger? ◆ If you could do anything with no obstacles in your way, what would you do?

- Where do you see yourself in five years?
- How would you like to be remembered?
- What would you want others to say about you when you're not listening?
- What do you want your contribution to be?

Step 7: Partner to Enhance Growth Between Sessions

Ask your coachee:

- How can you carry that perspective with you this week?
- What would remind you of that a-ha until we talk again?
- Can you try *[fill in]* this week?
- What assignment do you need to do to move you toward that goal this week?
- Will you take on this assignment? *[yes, no, or counteroffer]*

Step 8: Realign When Things Go Bad

Ask your coachee:

- What's stopping you?
- What are you avoiding? What aren't you saying?
- What do you feel is a roadblock to your success?
- Is this a perceived roadblock, or a real one?
- If you had unlimited resources and power, and there were no repercussions, how would you overcome this roadblock?
- What would be your next step?

continued on next page

STEP
6

Tool 6.2, continued

Step	Questions
	◆ What do you want to tell your gremlin?
	◆ What value are you stomping on right now?
Step 9: Maintain Positive Changes	*Ask your coachee:*
	◆ Where are you feeling satisfied/accomplished?
	◆ What will keep this feeling alive for you?
	◆ What is working?
	◆ What's possible for you right now?
Step 10: Complete the Coaching Cycle	*Ask your coachee:*
	◆ Is it time to complete our coaching relationship?
	◆ What did you learn?
	◆ What's next?
	◆ What do you want to celebrate about our work together?
	◆ Is there anything else you need to say right now before we part?
	◆ How should our relationship continue after the coaching is over?
	Ask yourself:
	◆ What did I learn by coaching this person?
	◆ Where did I grow as coach?
	◆ What questions do I have about coaching, and who can answer them?
	◆ What's next?

lot of coaching without knowing all the particulars, and it's only your own curiosity that wants to know all the gory details. Sometimes you seek the details because you want to build rapport and show an interest in the coachee's life. Remember that a little of that is fine, but manage yourself and your questions so that you're not bringing the conversation to a mundane level of minute detail. Here's what happens when you don't manage yourself:

Coachee: I think I need to move out of this city.

Coach: Really? How long have you been here?

Coachee: About 10 years. But it's just too expensive to raise a family here.

Coach: I know. How many children do you have?

Coachee: I have three.

Coach: That's nice. How old are they?

Coachee: Five, seven, and ten.

Coach: Nice ages. So, why do you think you have to move out of the city?

Although the coach might be interested in the number of children the coachee has and their ages, those details really aren't going to move this conversation forward and asking such questions is distracting the coachee from the situation. The coach is right to bring the conversation back around to the original issue—moving out of the city.

Here's how the conversation could have gone:

Coachee: I think I need to move out of this city.

Coach: What is it you're looking for that you don't have here?

Coachee: Well, it's really expensive to raise a family here.

Coach: So, you're looking for a place to live that's more affordable. What would that do for you?

Coachee: My wife and I wouldn't have to work as hard. We could relax more with our kids.

Coach: So you'd have more family time. What else would living in another area do for you?

Coachee: If we lived closer to the ocean, as I'd like to, we could be outside more and I could do more sailing, which I once loved to do. Haven't done it in a really long time.

Coach: OK. Let's talk about what moving would involve. And let's also talk about how you can get those things you're after—the family time, the sailing—right here and now without moving anywhere.

◆ **Close-ended questions.** You already know that open-ended questions are those that open the door for more talking, and close-ended questions require only a couple of words in response. But you may be surprised how often you use close-ended questions. When I started looking at this more closely, I was amazed how often I was shutting the door on valuable conversation. Here's where I got caught: As a trainer, I'd ask "Do you have any questions?" rather than "What questions do you have?" As a coach, I'd ask, "By when will you do that?" rather than "What's involved in getting that done?" As a parent, I'd ask "How was school today?" rather than "What was the funniest thing that happened at school today?" If people tend to respond to your questions with few words, consider how you're phrasing those questions and try again.

◆ **Leading questions.** These aren't really questions at all; they're statements posing as questions. They sound like this: "Don't you think you deserve a raise?" or "Are you a manager who frequently communicates with his employees?" Try not to manipulate questions to steer your coachee toward a certain belief or action.

◆ **Multiple questions.** I also call these run-on questions. Like run-on sentences, these questions just don't end. We heap on more and more questions because we're afraid we didn't ask it right the first time. Or our first question results in silence (and we all have a fear of silence), so we throw in another question to fill the space. People need time to consider their responses to your questions. They need to know what question they are being asked. Throw one out there and let it sit. If you do decide it was a bomb, break into the silence after several moments and just say, "I think that wasn't the right question. What question are you wanting to be asked about this right now?" Usually, however, simply sitting with the silence long enough will produce some real nuggets from the coachee. Remember that he's as uncomfortable with silence as you are, and to break the silence he's likely to contribute something he wasn't planning to talk about. At a minimum, he might say something like this: "That's not really the big question for me." That's your perfect opening for this response: "Great. What is the big question?"

How to Hear the Responses: Coach Listening

How do you need to listen when your coachee is telling you his biggest hopes and dreams? How do you need to listen to hear the greatness within him? I hope you see the value of good listening, rather than just thinking of it as a mechanical skill or as something you *should* do. How you listen to your coachee has a profound impact on his sense of self-worth and his ability to achieve.

So, how do you have to listen? The answer will be based partly on your designed relationship with your coachee. He may have told you he prefers positive input rather than being told what's going wrong. He may have said he needs time to vent and wants to know you're there to listen, rather than having you ask any questions. If you didn't have this conversation initially, you can ask at your next meeting, "How am I as a listener to you? What do you want more of or less of in my listening?" If you're not ready to have that discussion with your coachee, have it with your children or your siblings. They'll tell you. I hear it all the time: "Mom, I didn't want you to tell me what to do. I just wanted you to listen."

Make asking how you are expected to respond part of your everyday interactions. Try it at your next coaching session. Before you get under way, ask "What kind of response do you want from me after you share this?" Similarly, make it a practice to tell people what kind of listening and reaction you want from them. Doing so can circumvent a lot of difficult situations. For example, I asked a project team to do a practice presentation in front of my boss. I forgot to tell the boss that we really just wanted her overall opinion of how the senior management team might react to it. What we got was a critique that ripped the presentation apart piece by piece. I should have explained to her that although I was used to her feedback and could take it, this presentation was being made by a group of volunteers who'd worked really hard and who needed a little sugar-coating. I should have explained the purpose of her listening in on the practice session.

Beyond that, here's how I define the kind of listening you have to do as a coach. Coach listening is *briefly and in your own words reflecting the essence of the content and emotion the coachee is sharing.* Let's deconstruct that. We'll work with the following two examples:

- ◆ "My boss actually called me when I was on vacation last week. It made me so angry. She could have found what she was looking for herself. She tried to make it sound like she just needed me so much, that I'm indispensable, but really I felt she was just, once again, invading my private life."

- ◆ "My team members are so unmotivated, and I don't know what to do about it. I don't think you can teach work ethics or desire to do well. They either have it or they don't. What am I supposed to do with unmotivated people?"

Briefly means just that. If the coachee gives you a paragraph, you give him a sentence in a listening response. If he gives you a sentence, you give him a word. Here is a sentence for each of the examples above: "You're angry you had to work on your vacation," and "You don't think a boss can change the way people feel."

Reflecting what's been said **in your own words** is the best way to show that you've heard what your coachee has told you. Rephrasing shows you've internalized his message and made it your own.

Reflecting the essence means you're mirroring the most significant aspect of what the coachee has said, that which is at the heart of his statement. What's the essence in each of the two examples above?

After listening to the first speaker's message, I'd say he felt his personal time and space had been invaded, he'd been taken advantage of, or he was trapped. In the second example I notice feelings of being trapped again and of being inadequate and unable to perform. One thing to remember here: It's OK if you don't correctly identify your coachee's core message—he'll let you know if you're way off base. But simply by trying to capture the essence, you avoid unnecessary details and get more deeply into the real message.

Both **content and emotion** are important. Those of us who are thinkers or analysts (rather than feelers or emotional types) tend to focus on the content. We can be totally deaf to the emotion that's present in what someone is telling us. I learned this lesson the hard way while conducting a seminar for parents. I asked a parent for her impression of a book we'd just read. She gave a quick summary that was right on target. I said, "Thank you," and moved on. My co-leader said, "Wait, Sophie, I think Joan is really upset about what she read." I asked Joan if that was true. She nodded and began to cry. We ended up talking about the sadness that book created for her for quite some time. Many of the other participants had had similar reactions. A very rich conversation occurred because my co-leader noticed the emotion I missed in what Joan had been saying in her summary. That's a lesson I've carried with me ever since that seminar.

That brings up this fact: In coach listening, you do name the emotion. You don't ask, "How are you feeling?" You say, "You're angry that . . . " or "You're hurt that . . . ." Participants in my listening skills workshops often ask, "Aren't you just creating anger that way? Might he not get over it if you just moved on? Wouldn't your conversation in that group have been quicker and easier if you hadn't stopped him?" My answers? No—maybe—and yes. No, I'm not creating anger—just naming it. Maybe he would have gotten

STEP 6

over it and moved on, but is that what I want? To have him carry those sad feelings with him for the rest of the discussion? To have him think I didn't care? And then again, maybe he wouldn't have gotten over it. Then he wouldn't remain a productive member of our conversation; I'd have lost him and possibly others who felt as he did. And yes, it would have been quicker and easier just to gloss over his emotions, but that's not the goal in coaching. The goal is to peel the leaves off the artichoke to get at the heart inside, to remove all the layers your coachee has wrapped around himself that make him unable to access his solutions and magnificence. Naming the emotion and getting to the heart of an issue don't always mean taking lots of extra time. It only takes a moment to acknowledge that the coachee seems to feel sad or angry or discouraged.

When reflecting a speaker's feelings, you need a vocabulary of emotions. Repeatedly using the same words to describe someone's feelings grows stale and disingenuous over time. One way to develop a more comprehensive and accurate vocabulary to describe feelings is to read and reread a list of feeling words, like the one presented in tool 6.3. Add your own words to make this list more personally authentic.

Now taking another look at the two examples above, how would your coach listening responses sound?

Here are several responses that meet all the criteria—briefly and in your own words, reflecting the essence of the content and emotion the coachee is sharing:

- ◆ "It's annoying when you can't get away from your boss!"
- ◆ "You're fed up by having your privacy repeatedly invaded."
- ◆ "It's disappointing when your work ethic isn't shared."
- ◆ "You're stuck and confused about what to do with your team."

Having covered what coach listening is, let's consider what it is *not:*

- ◆ **Parroting**—How annoying it would be if you simply repeated what the coachee said. Do you hear the difference? The coachee says, "I'm tired of being micromanaged. She wants a list of steps and I don't work that way." A parroting response would be this: "So, you're tired of being micromanaged and want to do things your own way." A coach-listening response would sound more like this: "You want the trust of your boss to manage the way you know you can."

TOOL 6.3

Vocabulary of Emotions

Angry	Fearful	Happy	Inadequate
Irritated	Worried	Excited	Weak
Annoyed	Nervous	Joyful	Ineffective
Mad	On edge	Satisfied	Powerless
Frustrated	Scared	Glad	Vulnerable
Fed up	Frightened	Cheerful	Inept
Furious	Apprehensive	Up/high	Helpless
Infuriated	Panicked	Ecstatic	Small
Exasperated	Afraid	Energetic	Hopeless
Aggravated		Eager	
		Lively	
		Thrilled	
		Delighted	

Powerful	Sad	Stuck
Able	Low	Boxed in
Capable	Dissatisfied	Unsure
Effective	Glum	Confused
Competent	Depressed	Lost
Confident	Disappointed	Trapped
Dynamic	Unhappy	Struggling
Forceful	Upset	
Strong	Close to tears	

STEP 6

- **Advising/problem solving**—It's in our nature to want to help people. That's not a bad intention, but it is bad in coaching where you want people to access their own answers.
- **Turning the spotlight on you**—Coaching focuses on the coachee. Saying things like, "I know how you feel. I once had a boss who did this and that, and it always made me feel small" intrudes on that focus and makes it all about you.
- **Grading**—Whatever the coachee says has to be OK. Watch your facial reactions and your nonverbal communication. Do you display a poker face, or do you smile when they're "right" and frown when they're "wrong"? Do you sigh when they say something that disappoints you? Do you sit up straighter when they're talking about the stuff you like to hear? Even when I coach people on the phone, I try to keep myself from doing these things and I pay attention to the tone of my voice and the message it may convey. Of course, you want to refrain from verbal grading. That's when some of the things your coachee says get a response from you like "good" "great" or "a-ha," while others get a "tsk," a grunt, or no response at all. This isn't to say that a coach can't have a human response! It's just that there are some moments when the coach must be listening and not reacting. It is OK, however, to note your or the coachee's energy with a statement like, "When you talk about that, there's an electricity in the room. It got me sitting up straighter in my chair. How about you?"

Only after the coachee has been heard, when he's sorted out his feelings about the situation, will he be open to working on solutions. This is true even when he plainly asks for a solution, saying, "I'm so stuck. What should I do?"

Let's look at two possible conversations starting from the same place. In this first one, the coach makes a number of mistakes:

Coachee: I'm so stuck. What should I do?

Coach: Well, it seems like a talk with your manager is in order. *[giving solutions]*

Coachee: I've tried that over and over. Each time she seems to get it, but then it only lasts a week or so.

Coach: When was the last time you had one of these conversations? *[question about details; close-ended]*

Coachee: About a month ago. But it's hopeless. She's that way with everybody.

Coach: Has your whole team had a retreat lately? *[problem solving; close-ended]*

Coachee: Not for a couple of years.

Coach: I think a retreat is a great idea. I once worked for a manager like yours and a team retreat really turned things around. It's also a good way to bond outside the office, which you should be doing periodically anyway. *[spotlight on the coach; problem solving]*

Coachee: Well, OK.

Coach: Can you make that happen? *[close-ended question; leading question]*

Coachee: Yeah. . . .

Here's the second conversation, which shows a better coaching approach to the same opening statement:

Coachee: I'm so stuck. What should I do?

Coach: You seem at a loss for ideas.

Coachee: Yeah.

Coach: It's probably not very motivating to be scrutinized so closely all the time.

Coachee: Yeah, it's like I'm a kid and she's my disapproving Mom!

Coach: It's a dynamic that really makes you feel small.

Coachee: Yeah. And I've been doing this job for 12 years. I don't need to be told how to fill out a planning sheet.

Coach: It really irks you that your professionalism is continually called into question.

Coachee: Exactly.

Coach: You seem tired when you talk about this.

Coachee: I'm just bored. I feel like I've had this conversation again and again. I'm just tired of it.

Coach: It's probably disappointing to be back at this stage again.

Coachee: Yeah. Maybe I should start looking for a new job. But I love this job—or I did before she came along.

Coach: So, you want to fall in love with this job all over again.

Coachee: Yeah.

Coach: What can you do to fall back in love with your job, despite this boss?

Rather than leading the coachee, the coach has waited until she sensed that the coachee knew he'd been heard and was ready to move on. Then she shifted from listening to moving the discussion forward. Those two conversations came from the same situation, but they have very different energy and very different outcomes— all because of listening first.

One of my favorite parts of coaching is helping people see their own greatness. The world is big on pointing out our faults, but how often do we get to see how powerful we are? The days when coaching is most rewarding for me are those days when people realize something they saw as a far-off dream can happen now. There is magic in this step for coach and coachee alike.

Applying the Learning

◆ Who is your coachee at his core? Think about it and share it with him.

◆ Do you believe enough in your coachees/employees? Is there any area in which your opinion of what they're capable of doing is holding them back?

◆ Can you create more questions in your life? Ask four questions in every meeting this week, especially when someone asks you for advice. Notice if you're wedded to a certain response. What does that dynamic do for you?

◆ How do you want to listen? How does your coachee want you to listen? What parts of coach listening will be easiest for you? Which parts will be most difficult?

◆ As an argument is starting this week, pause and engage your coach listening skills. Instead of arguing your point, just reflect the essence of what your adversary has said. See how that turns the tide of the conversation. When it has de-escalated, you can return to your side of the situation at hand.

> **POINTER**
>
> Great work is done by people who are not afraid to be great. – *Fernando Flores, Chilean philosopher and politician*

STEP 6

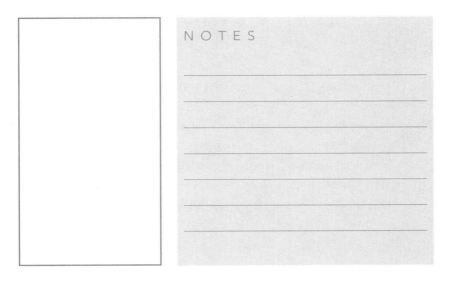

NOTES

STEP

6

Partner to Enhance Growth Between Sessions

There's a nightly negotiation in my house as my elementary school–aged children try to postpone doing their homework. "Why do we have to do homework?" they lament. "Why do you think you do?" I ask. And after their first response, which usually has the word "torture" in it somewhere, they give more informed answers, like "to practice what we learned that day," "to get us ready for a test," or "to show we know how to do it on our own."

Coaching "homework" is critical for the same reasons. When coachees complete assignments between sessions, they demonstrate— to themselves as well as to their coaches—that they're moving forward and can do so unaided. Assignments help coaches in their ultimate goal to create independence on the part of their coachees.

Additionally, assignments (simply anything that will keep a coachee's growth and development active and engaged between coaching sessions) help keep those sessions in the forefront of the coachee's thoughts and behaviors instead of in the background of the coachee's "real life."

STEP 7

The parallels between coaching homework and school homework end at their benefits, however. The way you completed assignments in school is very different from how you'll work with your coachee to enhance her growth between sessions. Tool 7.1 outlines these differences.

Let me expand a little bit more on each of the points highlighted in tool 7.1:

◆ **Partnering to create assignments**—The primary responsibility for achieving results through coaching is the coachee's. It follows, then, that the responsibility for com-

TOOL 7.1

How School Assignments and Coaching Assignments Differ

School Assignments	Coaching Assignments
Are created by the teacher.	Are co-created by the coach and coachee.
Are given to an entire class.	Are customized to—and accepted by—the coachee, with consideration for her goals, her situation, the time available to her, and a host of other factors.
Are routinely given every school night.	Are given as needed; never given just for the sake of having homework, but only to further the learning from a coaching session or progress toward a goal.
Are "doing" only—school assignments are all observable or tangible.	Coaching assignments can include nonobservable activities. For example, an assignment might ask the coachee to try behaving in a certain way with others and to notice the results of that behavior. Some coaching assignments are very subtle as the coachee simply tries out new beliefs or perspectives for herself.
Are graded.	There are no right answers to coaching assignments and no right (or wrong) way of completing them.
Are "torture" (ask a student!).	Are compelling; assignments are endeavors the coachee is motivated and excited to try.

ing up with the tasks and projects that will help her achieve them rests with her as well.

At the same time, it's often appropriate for the coach to suggest an assignment that he believes would help enhance the coachee's learning between sessions. In such situations, he should make sure that he's only suggesting, not mandating, the activity. Suggesting requires the use of language like "You might try . . . " or "I ask that you. . . . How does that sound?"

You must create a climate in which it's OK for coachees to say "no" to an assignment you suggest. If you have a more autocratic style and impose your ideas on your coachee, she may agree to do things she really doesn't want to do, and often she won't do them. Not following through is going to hamper the results that coaching can provide, and it does harm to the coachee's morale.

Later in this step, you'll find ideas for coming up with assignments together, as well as for starting a "storehouse" of assignment ideas on which you and your coachee can build.

◆ **Customizing the assignment and getting coachee acceptance**—Assignments can be work-related projects, thought-provoking questions, a new mantra, or anything else that helps the coachee continue to progress toward her goals. They will vary greatly in their complexity, length, and format. Factors that help determine what your coachee's assignments might look like include the coachee's style and interests, the focus topic, the time and resources available, and the desired outcomes.

How much work a coachee can take on between sessions is not for you to judge. Your coachees are adults who should learn to take on only what they can manage with their regular workload, outside concerns, and state of mind. It's your job only to create the relationship that is secure and open enough for them to tell you when they have reached their limits. It's interesting that many people who sign up for coaching are eager to receive assignments.

They tell me it makes them feel they're taking action in situations that have been hindering them. They're anxious to have control over such situations and they feel that assignments empower them to work on their issues.

Related to the issue of how much the coachee decides to take on is the issue of whether to cut her some slack when she's facing a tough situation outside of work. It's not up to you to stop offering assignments when the coachee has several personal issues going on. It remains her responsibility to consider how much she can take on at any given time. When she doesn't complete an assignment because of outside issues (at least those that were expected or already under way when she committed to the assignment), it's important to point out that she had the opportunity to turn down an assignment because of stressors in her life before she took it on. Doing so would have been preferable to not honoring her commitment. This may seem harsh, but it's a lesson better learned in a safe, supportive coaching situation than in a more demanding work situation where the stakes are higher.

I hope it was part of your initial relationship planning meetings to talk about "homework"—how much of it there will be, who will devise and complete all assignments, and what the coachee wants done when she doesn't complete the homework. Having all of those issues settled early in the process avoids conflict and misunderstandings at later sessions.

◆ **Giving assignments as needed**—Not every session needs to have an assignment, but remember that there's no forward movement between coaching sessions if there is no activity for which the coachee is responsible.

◆ **Doing and being**—I'd bet that most assignments you've been given in your life have been oriented around getting something done. Many coaching assignments are about "doing" something as well: completing a long overdue report, applying for a job, meeting with a problem employee, and so forth. But coaching assignments don't necessarily have that action-oriented, tangible target. Sometimes your coachee simply needs to think about an issue or a lesson, do some noticing or writing in her journal, mentally prepare for a tough meeting, take deeper breaths, or practice smiling more. These assignments are less transparent to the outside world and often more powerful and change producing than are the "doing" ones.

◆ **No right or wrong ways to complete an assignment—** Assignments created in this collaborative fashion may not look like any assignments you've given before—and that's OK. Additionally, when your coachee comes back to you the following session, she may not have completed her assignment in the way you imagined she would. Or after starting the assignment as designed, she may have found it didn't work for her and changed it. You may not have been allowed to do this in elementary school, but in coaching it's welcome. It means she considered the assignment and made it work for her. Now the assignment is more to her level, her interest, and her personal growth.

Although there's no right or wrong way to complete an assignment, I caution both coach and coachee to be careful about choosing the right assignment to be your starting point. Which assignment you and your coachee choose, or how you tweak the exercises you find to fit your coachee's focus topic, will depend on what outcome you and she desire.

The wrong assignment—one that doesn't address the coachee's desired outcome—can have harmful results. For example, let's say I instruct a coachee who's working on her budget to come to the next session with a draft of it for review. If she really isn't ready to produce a draft, that assignment could set her up for failure and/or sour her on future coaching assignments. In that scenario, I'd have been hoping for an outcome of movement, producing something, whereas the coachee's hoped-for outcome was finding the confidence just to get started. That disconnection is why assignments are best created in partnership so that the coachee's goal is served at every step. In that scenario,

a better assignment would have been something like finding two people who've created budgets successfully and
asking them what their first steps were. When the coachee
brought that information to the next session, we could
have talked about how she has accomplished those same or
similar steps for other types of projects. These are two very
different assignments producing two very different types of
outcomes.

◆ **Designing compelling assignments**—As you make a suggestion for a coaching assignment, be aware of your
coachee's spoken and unspoken responses. Usually you can
see or hear in her response when an assignment really
lights up her imagination and she's eager to try it. The
same is true when the idea falls flat and doesn't really appeal to her.

Realize that there is a difference between being hesi-
tant to take on an assignment and being unwilling or
uninspired by it. When an idea you had does seem to die,
ask your coachee what about that idea turns her off. If she
says something like "I've already tried that" or "That just
doesn't seem like something I'd want to do," your suggestion isn't an idea worth pursuing. But if her answer is more
like "I'd love to do that, but I don't know how I could" or
"I'd like to, but it scares me," it might be worthwhile to
tweak the idea a bit and challenge her to take it on. Some
people call these the juicy assignments: the ones that challenge coachees to do something they want to do, the ones
they can't wait to sink their teeth into, even if they have
some apprehension about doing so.

Even assignments that coachees "have" to do can be
made more juicy. As Tara and Evan Marcus propose in their
soon-to-be-published book *It's Okay to Play!*, you can turn
almost any task into a game. "When individuals find a
game that is a fit for them, it lights them up and they are
set free. Their energy is directed and purposeful. For example, when facing a daunting task, one game we suggest is
the Superhero game. In this game, you give yourself the

super powers needed to help you get the job done. Imagine taking on the day as Organized Woman or Unstoppable Selling Man! Pretending to be Super for the day sets a whole new level of intention and challenge."

And why do that? People are supposed to be at work; they get paid; why should their assignments be exhilarating? Tara Marcus adds, "Life is short, why not make it engaging? If we can take on challenges that help us professionally and that we value, they will more effectively help us become un-stuck and move forward. Why not take on something that makes us smile *and* helps us sail through our day?"

Finding Assignments

Say your coachee wants to run her first marathon and you've never even jogged around the block. How do you help her come up with an assignment that will help her achieve her goal? Where do you and your coachee get ideas for assignments or steps she should take when you might have no knowledge of the subject?

The good news is that ideas for exercises for your coachee are all around you. The first and most important place to look is within the coachee herself. She often will know what she needs to do in a given situation, and she simply has to be prompted to describe it and commit to doing it. So ask her, "What do people getting ready for marathons do?" or "What do you think your first step is? What comes after that?" or "Where can you go this week to get ideas for what steps to take?"

Often your coachee will name her assignment in the course of talking about her situation and move right on. You need to slow her down at these moments to get commitment to the assignment that's right under her nose. Here's how that might sound:

> **Coachee:** I've always wanted to apply for that fellowship. In fact, I really should just go ahead and do it. Fellowships are important and so is writing articles. I have a friend who wrote an article and got three job offers afterward.

I've heard that the good journals are always looking for..."

Coach: Whoa! You've just mentioned two possible assignments for yourself. Are these things you want to commit to doing?

Coachee: What assignments? What do you mean?

Coach: I heard you say you wanted to apply for a fellowship and to write an article.

Coachee: I did? I guess I did. But I can't do both those things. And I don't even know what fellowships are out there.

Coach: OK. Can you figure out which ones are out there before we talk again? Is that something you want to do?

Coachee: I guess so. I guess I could at least start...

Coach: Could you come back with three possible fellowships next time?

Coachee: Sure.

Coach: What about the article? What kind of information about writing an article could you start looking for this week?

Coachee: Well, I would need to find a topic... and know which publications are out there... and what they're looking for....

Listen for the "shoulds" in your coachee's conversation. When you hear one, turn it into an assignment. If she says, "I should get a first draft done by next week," say, "OK, will you?" If she says, "I'd like to start a website business on the side, but I don't know where to get the funding," say, "Can you find out by next week?" Another way to elicit assignments from the coachee is to ask questions like these: What assignment do you want to be working on? or For what other action do you want me to hold you accountable between now and the next time we talk? When she doesn't propose an assignment idea, you can say, "I feel like you should be doing something this week to move you closer to your goal. What is it?"

What if your coachee can't think of a suitable assignment to move her toward her goal? Where else can you and she go for assignment ideas? The supermarket, the bookstore, the computer, the sports arena, or her workplace, to name a few. At the supermarket, you'll find magazines loaded with ideas for self-improvement. Consider some recent articles in *O Magazine,* for instance: "Have Your Own A-ha Moment," "Live Your Best Love Life," and "Look at Your Life." Those articles suggested myriad assignments that readers could complete on their own to achieve the lives they're seeking.

The self-help aisle of the bookstore is also a fun place to shop for ideas. Even books that are ubiquitous in pop culture (and thus somewhat suspect in my eyes) contain usable gems. Take Rhonda Byrnes' international bestseller *The Secret* (Atria Books, 2006). Whether or not you subscribe to the author's theories 100 percent, it's hard not to relate to the concept that thinking positively will bring you positive results. The business aisle has books on leadership, management, and a number of other specific topics that might contain exercises suitable for coaching. Books of training activities can be adapted easily for coaching.

On the Internet, you just need to do a Google search for coaching exercises and list a topic. You'll be connected to hundreds of ideas that other coaches are selling or giving away. Even blogs written for inspirational thinkers and speakers (like Daryn Kagan's blog, which aims to "show the world what's possible") are rife with ideas (www.darynkagan.com).

Old training manuals and binders provide another assignment source right in the workspace. The exercises trainers use in workshops or presentations were great when you first learned them, and they still are.

Even looking at drills that sports coaches use can spur a creative assignment for your coachee. For instance, if a basketball coach has all players line up, shoot a basket, and run to the back of the line, you and your coachee might create a similar assignment for her to use with her team (each member throws out an idea and goes to the back of the line) or in her personal brainstorming sessions (she gets out of her chair and adds some sort of energizing movement).

Say your coachee is working on time-management issues. Here are assignments you might come up with just by using all of the techniques I've listed above:

◆ **At the supermarket**—Ask your coachee to watch for time-management techniques that people in the store are using and then to think about how she could use those techniques in the workplace. For instance, people are using shopping lists (truly serious shoppers have organized their lists according to where things are located in the store), some are reading the newspaper or their mail in the checkout line, some shut off their cell phones now that they're off the job (there's learning in this—ask your coachee what she had to do to shut off her cell phone), and others place orders in the meat department and shop while the orders are prepared. When asked how to apply some of these techniques to her workplace, one of my clients suggested making to-do lists that group all calls to return in one area, all emails to write in another, and so forth.

◆ **At the bookstore**—The first book that caught my eye when I was on the prowl for time-management coaching exercises was Jeffrey Mayer's bright yellow *Time Management for Dummies* (1999). Its first section includes a test of one's time-management savvy that would be a great starting point for your coachee with time-management issues.

◆ **On the Internet**—A quick Google search for "free time-management exercises" took me to Patricia Katz's Optimus Consulting website (www.patkatz.com) where I found this free exercise:

Choose three tasks that you'll be working on this week. Write down your estimate of how long each task will take to complete. As you work on these tasks, track the real time spent on each one. At the end of the week, compare your estimates with the actual results. If you were within 20 percent of your estimate, congratulations. If you were beyond or below the 20 percent mark, look for reasons why you might have over- or underestimated the time required. Use your insights to adjust your estimates on next week's projects. To improve your ability to estimate required task times, repeat this exercise weekly for one month.

◆ **In old training binders**—A time-management workshop I went to a dozen years ago included an exercise in which participants put all of their activities into a grid (like the one in example 7.1).

◆ **From a sports coach**—Because I was on the lookout for coaching exercises having to do with time management, I was intrigued by something I saw in a televised football game. How those coaches used their time-outs was a time-management strategy that my coachees could use. I asked one of my clients how he could use a time-out exercise in the workplace. He came up with the obvious: He would take one time-out each working day and use it as the athletes do—to plan strategy, to rest, or just to get a drink of water.

◆ **In the workplace**—One time-management exercise that coachees can try in their workplace is pulling out or printing their calendars and doing an analysis: How many of the meetings they had in a day were scheduled, compared with how many were unplanned? How many were "one-time" meetings, compared with the number of routine meetings? How many started late?

Remember, these aren't necessarily tips for you, the coach, to employ. They're also sources you can share with your coachee so that she can find her own coaching assignments. My point here is that you must not feel that you have to come up with all of the assignments, just as you don't have to come up with all the answers. First and foremost, it is the responsibility of the coachee to decide what needs to be done. Rather than scouring the shelves or the websites yourself for exercises appropriate to your coachee's issues, send the coachee to those sources between sessions so she can create her own assignments.

Going with exercises that someone else (including your coachee) has suggested or published is not a sign of your weakness as a coach;

STEP **7**

EXAMPLE 7.1

Time-Management Grid

Coachee instructions: Identify a group of tasks you must complete. Decide if each one is urgent or not urgent, and then if it is important or not important. Write each task in the appropriate box on the grid. You may put more than one task in any box. When you've sorted all the tasks, challenge yourself to

- Do those that are both urgent and important first.
- Remove from your plate those tasks that are both not urgent and not important.
- Delegate some of the tasks that are urgent but not important.
- Make those tasks that are important but not urgent more urgent by imposing artificial deadlines on them and then scheduling time in your day to work on them. If you break this "appointment" and don't get these things done, reschedule them as you would any other priority.

	Urgent *These tasks have deadlines or there is some immediacy to getting them done*	**Not Urgent** *There are no looming deadlines by which these tasks need to be completed*
Important *These tasks will have a significant impact on your work or on the organization; these tasks are meaningful*		
Not Important *These tasks are not going to have a significant impact in your workplace; they aren't valuable in the long run*		

it's a model of using your existing resources to great advantage. Once you realize that coaching exercises are all around you, setting up an idea storehouse where you can capture them is a great idea. You'll have these exercises ready when you and your coachee feel stuck. My storehouse is a binder divided by topic area, with a page for each exercise. Yours can be a computer database or index card file. However you format it, it's a great way to remember the good exercises you've come across. Even the act of writing them down or copying them for your storehouse helps put these activity ideas into your long-term memory so you can pull one out when you need it.

Here are some exercises from my storehouse that are connected to certain desired outcomes I've encountered repeatedly in my coaching. Use them to jump-start the creation of your own storehouse.

Assignments for Remembering

These are the assignments whose outcomes are to help coachees stay connected to a great new perspective or to a breakthrough she's had during a coaching session. For instance, your coachee might have realized during the session that giving regular feedback to her direct reports is a gift to them, not a punishment or a chore. Perhaps you both really want her to remember that realization during the coming week. Here's how that conversation might go:

> **Coach:** That sounds like a new way to look at this situation.
>
> **Coachee:** Yeah. I always thought employees pretty much dreaded these performance review meetings.
>
> **Coach:** So, during the coming week, how do you want to remember that what you're giving them—a clear vision of how they're performing—actually is a rare opportunity?
>
> **Coachee:** I guess I could just start out the meetings by giving them this perspective and helping them understand where I'm coming from with my feedback. That I just want to hold a mirror up for them to show them how they come across.
>
> **Coach:** And how will you remember to do that?
>
> **Coachee:** Oh, I just had an idea. This may sound corny, but what if I put a little mirror in my desk drawer this week so that when I open it to pull out their files for the meeting, I'll be reminded?

Remembering assignments often involves some sort of visual reminder, like a sticky-note on the computer, a job aid, a poster on the wall, or a tickler in the coachee's calendar. Help your coachee figure out what visual reminders she can place in her environment to recall what she's trying to accomplish and who she's trying to be. One of my former bosses had on her desk a collection of turtle figurines from all over the world. They reminded her to slow down. There also were some unanticipated benefits to the collection: We respected her for admitting to her tendency to move too quickly, and for being vulnerable in front of us. Over the years, the whole team added to the collection with turtles we found on business trips and vacations. That became a sort of unifying activity.

Assignments for Thinking About a Topic

These are assignments in which your coachee simply needs to spend more time considering an idea or a question between sessions. Here's how the assignment conversation might go:

> *Coachee:* I'm not that kind of a supervisor. I don't think I should have to check in with my employees to see if they're doing what they said they were doing. That's hand-holding, and my employees are adults!

> *Coach:* You raise a big question there, you know? When you say you're not the hand-holding kind of supervisor, it begs the question, "What kind of supervisor are you?"

> *Coachee:* Well, I'm conscientious, I'm organized, I push my employees but they respect me. I . . .

> *Coach:* Let me interrupt with a Dr. Phil–type question: How's that working for you?

> *Coachee:* Well, you know, it's not going too well . . .

> *Coach:* So, what kind of supervisor do you want to be?

> *Coachee:* I don't know—effective, motivating . . .

> *Coach:* Is this something you want to think about some more this week?

> *Coachee:* Yeah. I can see how it would be important to know that.

> *Coach:* So how will you keep thinking about this?

STEP **7**

Coachee: Well, I keep a journal. I can write about it every night.

Coach: Great. And will you send me an overview of your thoughts—not the entries themselves, unless you want to—before we talk again?

When asking your coachee to consider something, you might just ask her to set aside 10 minutes a day to sit with the question and think about it. It takes some time to come up with really meaty answers to meaty questions. Some of my clients carry with them for a week a written version of the question or idea they want to mull over so that whenever they have a spare moment, or come across it in the course of their ordinary activities, they can think about it. I've also had clients prepare mini-presentations on ideas or decisions that they're considering.

Assignments for Noticing

These are assignments in which your coachee heightens her awareness of something between sessions: "Monitor your reaction when you're in meetings with that person," "Notice how fast your heart is beating when that type of situation arises," or "Count how many interruptions you have in one work day." Again, you can ask the coachee to journal about what she notices, send you an email, or just keep a chart with tally marks for every time she noticed what she meant to notice. Noticing often involves objective observing— for example, counting the number of meetings on her calendar or the number of nights she made it home in time for dinner, or tracking time spent on particular projects.

Many of my clients tell me that the biggest thing they've gotten out of coaching is that they're noticing more. They notice when they're unhappy so they can take action to improve their circumstances. They're noticing and celebrating when they've reached a milestone or experienced a success. Noticing is a simple but extremely powerful tool, and I urge coaches and coachees alike to find ways and times to slow down or sit still and notice what's happening for them.

STEP 7

By the way, your body is a great place to notice what's happening for you at any given moment. We hold our stress and our heartaches in our bodies. Our heart rates tell us when we're rushed or pressured. We feel in our gut when we're doing something that conflicts with our values or ethics. Our illnesses tell us when we're not getting enough sleep or working too hard. We often remain out of touch with what our bodies are telling us until it's too late and we're really suffering. Checking in with your coachee on whether she's having some bodily (physical) reaction to a certain situation is a terrific way for both of you to learn what's really happening.

Assignments for Enlisting Resources

This is the assignment to embark on when your coachee needs some expertise that neither you nor she possesses, as in this situation:

> *Coach:* You say you'd like to increase your market share. When have you had an opportunity to do this in the past?
>
> *Coachee:* I really haven't. I was hoping you'd have some ideas for me about how to do it.
>
> *Coach:* That isn't really my specialty either. But my specialty is helping you figure out who has that expertise so you can get the information you need.
>
> *Coachee:* Great. Where do I go?
>
> *Coach:* Well, where were you thinking of going?
>
> *Coachee:* My boss suggested I talk to the Chamber of Commerce. They might have some ideas about the local marketplace, and I think they also offer workshops on this topic from time to time.
>
> *Coach:* What do you think of your boss's idea?
>
> *Coachee:* To tell you the truth, I've found the Chamber workshops to be a little simplistic.
>
> *Coach:* Whose sophisticated ideas do you really admire?
>
> *Coachee:* About market share?
>
> *Coach:* Sure. Who's expanded his or her own market share in an impressive way?

Coachee: Hmmm. My friend works for the community college system, and she helped them capture more of the market so students would take classes through the college rather than through private vendors.

Coach: Great. She's someone you can talk to about this.

Coachee: Yeah. I guess . . .

Coach: So, will you?

Coachee: I don't know. I haven't spoken to her in a long time and . . .

Coach: OK. If not her, what about asking the Chamber of Commerce who in the area has seen his or her business really grow and then contacting that person to find out how he or she made that happen?

Coachee: I hadn't thought about that. I guess they'd know some of the local success stories.

Coach: So is that who you need to talk to this week—local business owners who've been successful? Will you call three of them this week and ask them for 10–15 minutes of their time to learn about what worked for them? Incidentally, people love to share their successes and to be called on for their expertise. Is this something you can do?

Coachee: Sure. That feels a lot better than asking them what I should do, like asking for free advice. I just contact them and ask them to share their stories with me.

This coach started by discussing resources that already had been considered. Then he asked his coachee to pin down what type of people she wanted to speak with, and he gave her a new way to approach those resources. In the end, a tangible assignment was agreed on. Keep that conversation in mind for when you and your coachee need the input of some subject matter experts.

Assignments for Just Doing It

Coaching is a safe and comfortable relationship that should encourage people to go out and try new or risky things. A coachee should know that her coach has complete confidence in her, and that if she isn't successful, her coach will be there to help her sort out the pieces. If your coachee feels that way about your coaching relationship, it might be time simply to give her a challenge and push her out there to do it. When her job requires her to do something that's a stretch, when she's talked about doing something for a long time but been slow to get started, or when there's something she really wants to do that she keeps talking herself out of, it's time to give her a "sink-or-swim" assignment.

In their book *Eighty-Eight Assignments for Development in Place* (CCL Press, 1989), Michael M. Lombardo and Robert W. Eichinger posit that challenge and growth can be added to anyone's job within an organization. They cite five kinds of opportunities that are developmental: (1) putting people into challenging jobs, (2) having them work with people other than those they're used to (mostly bosses), (3) enduring a hardship, (4) taking courses (particularly ones in which they can interact with others at their level or in their industry), and (5) creating off-the-job experiences that would give them the skills they're seeking back at work.

A coach can help his coachee locate an assignment like these that would give the coachee the growth opportunities she's seeking. Of course, he'll have to help her as she fumbles and experiments her way through it. Says Chris Emery (remember that coach-like manager from Step 1?), "I shift people into a blend of responsibilities that may fit or digress from their traditional roles. I let them work on some things that are in their self-described 'comfort zone,' and then I ask them to participate in activities and projects that provide them with a personal 'gut check.' If you never test someone, you will never know how high she can jump, or where she will land."

There are some things I ask clients to just go out and *do,* and there are other things I ask them to *experiment with.* Experimenting is an especially useful practice when it comes to adopting new ways of being or interacting. When coachees face giving up something they like or that's comfortable for them or integrating something new and difficult into their lives, it's often more manageable if they think about doing it as a short-term experiment rather than adapting it for all time. I see people fail more often when they're told to change the way they behave indefinitely than when they're told to do it for one week—and then maybe one more week, and then maybe one week after that. I phrase most of my assignments as experiments now because sometimes it makes failure more tolerable and less damaging. With an experiment, we simply can design a new one and try again. It's less of an absolute way of approaching a situation. Examples of short-term activities that a coachee surely can manage for a week include stopping by everyone's desk to say "hello" in the morning, using only positive language, working from home, providing recognition to one person a day, or blocking off time on her calendar for nonwork activities that she should not reschedule.

> POINTER
>
> Great ability develops and reveals itself increasingly with every new assignment. –
>
> Baltasar Gracian, 17th century Spanish writer

It should be pointed out that there is some noticing that goes with experimenting (How did it work? How did you feel? What about it do you want to repeat?), but the most important thing is that you just create a space in which your coachee is willing to try something new for a short period of time.

By completing assignments on their own between coaching sessions, coachees learn what they're capable of doing and reinforce what they've learned. Coaching assignments differ from other types of assignments because they are co-created, accepted, ungraded, and compelling. Devising exercises for coaching takes creativity and resourcefulness, as well as a willingness to let go and see how things work. Without assignments, coachees will make limited movement toward their goals.

Applying the Learning

◆ Pick up a self-help book or magazine this week. Find two coaching exercises in it, and use them to start your idea storehouse.

◆ Find out what outcomes your coachee wants this week. What assignments might elicit those outcomes?

◆ With your coachee, devise one or two juicy assignments to complete by her next session.

NOTES

Realign When Things Go Bad

Many appliances and electronic products come with troubleshooting guides—those charts that list things that could go wrong and a few suggestions for fixing them. It's unfortunate that in coaching, as in life, the troubleshooting guide isn't included. And, to be honest, that probably makes a lot of sense. Have you ever heard a strangling sound coming from the dishwasher and checked that list of possible glitches, hoping to find "strangling noise" so that you can get your solution and move on? I bet it wasn't there. No list can contain all of the different ways that your appliance might malfunction. In the same way, there's no way to anticipate and plan to counteract all the ways that coaching might get derailed.

In this step, we'll consider ways to identify and treat problems (whether simmering or at full boil) that may arise in your coaching relationships—at least, the more common problems. Let's start with deciding if things are going bad.

STEP **8**

Is It Bad?

The following list probably misses some of the unique snags you'll experience in coaching. Or maybe you're hitting several of these potholes already and at once. That said, here are a few telltale signs that you're in a coaching rut:

◆ **It's getting difficult**—You're starting to dread your coaching sessions or each one is a struggle.

◆ **The agenda keeps changing**—Your coachee can't focus on what he wants; new issues surface week after week and there is no apparent theme.

◆ **It's sounding like a broken record**—You've heard the coachee complaining about the same issues, or using the same excuses, or just saying the same thing over and over; you'd describe the coaching as being at a standstill.

◆ **It's boring**—You have trouble staying connected and listening actively in your coaching sessions because it's just downright dull.

◆ **It's superficial**—Your conversation is only skimming the surface; the coachee stays at a very uninvolved or unemotional level and doesn't seem willing to explore the situation more deeply.

◆ **Your coachee is still thinking small**—You simply can't get the coachee to expand his vision of what he's capable of; he continually rejects stretch assignments or creates a vision that is uninspiring to himself and others.

◆ **Resistance and defensiveness enter the coaching**—A formerly engaged and willing coachee starts to challenge you as his coach or becomes defensive.

If you recognize any of these signs from your own coaching relationships, congratulations! Yup, I said congratulations. Why? First, you've noticed that things have gone awry in your relationship, and recognizing is a skill in itself. Second, you now have a chance to really deepen your coaching relationship and expand what's possible for your coachee. It is often in adversity that we learn the most about ourselves and our relationships. It's like when you're first dating someone new. You're deliriously happy, and your wise best friend asks, "But have you had your first argument yet?" She knows that it isn't until you've worked through your first conflict that you truly know how this relationship might hold up. It may be stronger or it may collapse, and a lot can be learned from seeing just how that plays out.

Granted, the rocky period when some cracks are showing in the coaching may not feel like a time to celebrate, but knowing that this is a time for great growth can be a good way to enter this step in the process. It's bound to come for everyone.

The Unspoken Truth

I mentioned how great it is just to realize when things are going downhill. One of the skills that's used to do that is the skill of listening to what's not being said. For a coach, listening is more than framing reflections, as described in Step 6; it's also being very aware of what's going on in the bigger environment. You have to be able not only to listen closely to the coachee, but also to pull yourself out of that conversation and look at it from the fly-on-the-wall vantage point. From that distance you get to see how the third party in the room is doing—that is, your relationship. As you'd expect, a skill like this takes practice.

To hone your ability to hear what's not being said, during the next meeting you're attending where you are not directly participating, stop listening to the words being said for a moment and tune in to the energy in the room. Are people engaged, listless, wanting something more? What can you tell about the participants' relationships just by the tone of their voices and their body language? You don't have to spend the whole meeting in this zone; just practice visiting it now and then to get a sense of what's not being said. You also can try to achieve the same awareness in conversations with friends and family members. Perhaps then you might practice commenting on what you're observing: "Did you notice the high energy level in the room when that vendor was talk-

STEP **8**

ing to us? People were nodding and smiling. I'd say she really engaged us," or "Your tone of voice with your sister was a little crisp
during breakfast this morning. I sensed a tension between the two
of you. Anything going on?"

Looking Within for Fixes

Where do you think realigning starts in a coaching relationship
that's "gone bad"? Like most of coaching, it begins with you. A re-
lationship is a reflection of both parties involved—as the coach, you're not ex-cluded from doing some thinking and work to turn the situation around.

Your gremlins are the first place to check in with yourself. Are any of the following voices present? "I don't know enough about this." "Who am I to be coaching this person?" "He can't possibly make all this happen in his life." Once again, it's time to notice and name these gremlins and to decide what you want to do with them in this coaching relationship.

POINTER

Remember these techniques for taming your gremlins:

- Recognize that these voices are stating beliefs, not facts, and that beliefs can be changed.
- Notice and name your gremlins.
- Decide what's true about the gremlin's message and be grateful for it.
- Decide what's untrue about the gremlin's message.
- Decide whether you want to honor and live by what the gremlins are saying, or honor and live by what is drawing you to try something new. In other words, is what your gremlin is saying more important than whatever is calling you to change?
- Decide what you want to do with the gremlin—heed its advice, shut it up (literally or figuratively), journal about it, sit with it, and so forth.

Here's how taming your gremlins might sound at this step. Let's say this gremlin voice is impeding your ability to coach effectively: "He's never going to make this change; this is use-less!" Start by remembering that it's just a belief and, if you want to, you can work to change it. You might recognize the truth in it— that if coaching continues as it has been, it is useless. How lucky that you've noticed and can turn your sessions into something more valuable. Do you want to honor the voice that says, "He's never going to make this change," or the one that says, "I can coach through his resistance and help him make changes that will really make a world of positive difference for him?" This gremlin might just be the impetus for shaking up your coaching and getting your coachee back on track.

Another personal place to explore has to do with how you feel about your coachee. Let's be honest here. Some people who report to you but whom you don't especially like may need a coach. You may have angry or negative feelings toward some of the people coming to you for help. When it's part of your job to coach all the people who seek your help, you have no say in who that will be. But when respecting and caring for your coachee is key, when you really need to enjoy and want the very best for your coachee, can you have an effective coaching relationship with someone you don't respect or like? Here are some questions to consider in identifying your feelings toward your coachee:

- What is it about *you* that makes it hard to like this person? Which of your buttons does he press? What does he bring out in you that you don't especially like? What self-management is necessary to change your reaction to him?
- Why can't you want the very best for him? Would his success mean that he'd surpass you professionally? Is that OK? If you don't want your coachee to perform or achieve at his very best, this isn't a good coachee for you.
- What would he need to do to earn your respect? Figure this out and share it with him. You're working not only to improve the situation your coaching is in; you're also modeling how to request what you need.

After doing your own work, if you think this person isn't a good fit with you, for whatever reason, it might be time to suggest a new coach for him and to jump ahead to Step 10.

STEP 8

Finally, there are going to be times when issues in your personal life draw your attention during a coaching session or make coaching difficult. Make it a regular practice to ground yourself before each coaching session, especially at times when the coaching is not going well. How do you ground yourself? Take a few minutes before the coaching session to get in a coaching frame of mind. Turn on voicemail and close the door, review your notes from the prior coaching session. Think about anything going on for you that might get in the way of coaching and decide what you want to do about it. Is it so all-consuming that you want to reschedule your session? Can you set an intention to be there for the coachee and to come back to your pressing concerns after the session?

Be honest with your coachee at the start of his session about what's happening for you. When you're not honest about this, your coachee may think that he's doing something wrong. When he can't figure out what's "off" during a particular coaching session, he'll blame himself. Disclose for him when something is going on in your life, as you'd want the coachee to do for you. For example, "I'm here today to listen to you and guide you as I always am, but I'm also worried about my father who has pneumonia and is in the hospital. I'm not telling you this for sympathy or so you'll 'go easy on me' today. I just thought I should let you know this is happening because it's present for me."

> POINTER
>
> Failure is the opportunity to begin again, more intelligently.
>
> – Henry Ford, industrialist

Realigning

The point in a coaching relationship where things go off the rails is the point that most new coaches fear—partly because they see this as a period of conflict and they're generally conflict-averse. To the contrary, I choose to see it as a period of realigning and to think how lucky we are that we have the opportunity in these relationships to realign. If only we could realign our families, our government, or our finances so easily.

So, how to make the most of this opportunity? Overall, you want to keep it positive. Make sure your coachee knows how much you value your relationship and how much you value him. Explain that all relationships hit rocky points and that the work you do at those difficult times has real potential to move him along and to produce deeper results. Remind him of the agreements you reached in Step 3, and get his commitment now to work through this with you.

In keeping it positive, you may have to steer the focus away from blaming. Sure there are things he could be doing better as a coachee, you might have to say, and things you could be doing better as a coach. This isn't about blaming; it's simply about creating a rewarding relationship. So the focus you're going to choose to take is "what can we do from here?"

Humor helps keep the situation light. If you can have a good time together as you work through your difficult periods, that's great. For example, you can play up his gremlin, exaggerate it so he can hear how silly it is. Doing so might sound like this: "Oh, right, I forgot, you can't motivate your employees because you are just so dull. You don't have it in you to inspire others. Right?"

If you're the coachee's manager, some of the options that are always available to you when times get tough for one of your employees can be expended on your coachee. For example, you can

- ask him what kind of support he'd find helpful
- provide resources for him to solve this problem, possibly including training or education
- provide time for him to do his coaching assignments, perhaps by reprioritizing his work
- (with his permission) let others know he's working on this goal so that he gets the time and space he needs from co-workers
- make connections on his behalf
- praise his progress at milestones
- consider providing an incentive when he achieves his desired results.

STEP 8

Troubleshooting Guide

Even though I've railed against the troubleshooting guides that most appliance manufacturers create, there are a lot of tips I've picked up for some of those common problem areas that crop up now and again (emphasis on *again*) in coaching. Like those appliance guides, this section won't present a comprehensive list of everything that can go wrong, nor of every possible solution, but it can be looked at as a place to start—as a simple jumping-off point.

Your Coachee Repeatedly Says, "I Don't Know"

My first coaching mentor, Caryn Siegel, taught me this amazing tip for addressing just such a situation: To the coachee who laments, "I don't know," simply say, "What would you say if you did know?" Somehow this question frees people to use their imaginations. It's like saying, "If you don't know, take a guess"—an approach that gives people the freedom to get it wrong. They can then answer theoretically, rather than in some way that they'll be held to, and they access answers they claim not to know.

Another way to address this problem is to ask the coachee to think of a time when he did know what to do in a similar situation, or ask, "What would you tell a friend in the same situation?"

Your Coachee Says, "You're the Coach— You Tell Me!"

This is the time to remind your coachee of the coach's role, which is not to give advice but to help him find the answers he has inside him. I usually phrase it this way: "I could give you my answer, but that would only be mine and might not work for you. What do you think needs to be done?"

I won't lie, however, and tell you that I never respond to this question with my own answer, especially when I have some expertise in the problem with which my client is struggling. In those situations, I either say, "I can answer that for you at the end of our

STEP **8**

session, but I don't want my answer to cloud yours. First I'd like to hear how you would approach it" or "I'm going to step out of my role as a coach for a minute and tell you something I've learned in my years of being in your situation. Is that OK with you?" Being a coach does not mean you have to relinquish your role as a subject matter expert; it just alters the way you present that expertise. Remember, you are responding this way to help create independence, rather than dependence, on the part of your coachee.

Your Coachee Is a Glass-Half-Empty Person

Some coachees have a pessimistic perspective that isn't easy to shake. When that's the case, I often start coaching with a question about what it's like for him to have such a perspective not just at work but in all aspects of his life. I ask what might be possible for him if he tried another perspective, such as "This is perfect" or "I choose to think positively about this situation."

There also are some clients I let stew in their negative perceptions until we come to a place where it sounds ridiculous even to them. I start with the classic "What's the worst that can happen?" question, but I don't stop there. I keep asking, "And then what?... And then what?... And then what?"

> *Coach:* So, what's the worst thing that can happen?
>
> *Coachee:* I'll totally bomb this speech.
>
> *Coach:* And then what?
>
> *Coachee:* Well, then I'll be embarrassed—and in front of my boss.
>
> *Coach:* And then what?
>
> *Coachee:* And then we won't get the client and it'll look really bad on my record.
>
> *Coach:* And then what?
>
> *Coachee:* I won't get promoted again and no one will want to be on my team.
>
> *Coach:* And then what?
>
> *Coachee:* And then I'll be unhappy.

STEP **8**

Coach: And then what?

Coachee: Well, I'll want to quit.

Coach: And then what?

Coachee: I guess I'll either quit and get a new and better job, or I won't quit and people eventually will forget about it.

Your Coachee Just Doesn't Want to Do Something

As coaches, we try to get our coachees to focus on tasks that bring them energy, joy, or fulfillment. We don't want their goals and tasks to be driven by "should" or "have to"—by reasons that don't inspire them or enhance their growth. However, there are certainly times that coachees have to commit to doing things they don't want to do or that they keep putting off. How do you help coachees do those things they must but don't want to do? With their agreement, I often resort to bribery or punishment in such situations. I use the motivators we covered in Step 5 to reward the coachee, or I ask him to impose consequences on himself if he doesn't do what he committed to do. One client wanted to write a budget but had put off doing it for a long time. We agreed that there needed to be some incentive for him finally to complete it. We decided that he would pay $50 to the charity of my choice for every week he was late in getting the work done. This incentive/ punishment was his idea because he said he hated to lose money (so it would be motivating for him to avoid it), and if he did have to pay, someone would benefit.

Maybe you'd rather not go the route of reward and punishment. Example 8.1 offers instead a terrific exercise that helps your coachee discover that doing even the most dreaded activities really is a choice he makes for a reason that's meaningful to him. Suggest that he complete the exercise and then make special effort to notice what, if anything, changes for him when he's doing the tasks he's listed. Does knowing the actual reason behind his choosing to do them make a difference? Also suggest to your coachee that he review the list to identify trends—how many of the tasks listed

EXAMPLE 8.1

Choosing My Actions

Coachee instructions: In the center column below, list things that you don't experience as fun, that you don't enjoy doing. Use the active (present tense) voice. Example: *Attend weekly staff meetings.* Notice the words "I choose to . . . " in the first column. Those words will help you realize in a way you didn't before that you're making a choice, that the activities in the second column really aren't being imposed on you—you are choosing to do them for a reason that is meaningful to you. That's where the third column comes in: For each activity you've listed, write why you choose to do it. Continuing with the example above, *I choose to attend weekly staff meetings because I want to be an active member of this team [or to enhance workplace communication, or because I want to be in the know].* Be sure the reasons you place in the third column are meaningful to you, not merely words you think you *should* be writing there.

	Activities I don't enjoy	Meaningful Reason for Doing It
I choose to . . .		
I choose to . . .		
I choose to . . .		
I choose to . . .		
I choose to . . .		
I choose to . . .		

Source: Adapted from and used with permission of Marshall B. Rosenberg, *Nonviolent Communication: A Language of Life* (Encinitas, CA: PuddleDancer Press, 2003, www.nonviolentcommunication.com).

STEP 8

there are done for others and how many is he doing for himself, how many have severe consequences if he doesn't do them, how many are done for financial reasons or to avoid conflict? Those are valuable insights to have when making significant changes.

Your Coachee Is Stuck

When your coachee complains about being stuck, it's usually partnered with a strong belief about what he has to do in a situation or what is expected of him (for example, "I should be closer to completion on this project, but I'm just not getting anywhere"). These beliefs sometimes are stale or incorrect, but he'll hold on to them because he doesn't see that there are any other choices. Try some questions like "Is that true?" "What if it's not true?" "Is the opposite also true?" "If it's true, what opportunities are present?"

To help your coachee get unstuck, help him try another perspective—maybe even one that seems totally unrelated to his problem. Here's an exercise for that:

1. Have your coachee state his problem (for instance, "I'm in a dead-end job") and set it aside.
2. Ask him to think of another unrelated topic—say, cooking—and for four minutes jot down everything he can about the new topic (such as preheat the oven, buy fresh ingredients, measure carefully).
3. Ask him to consider what items on his cooking list can apply to his original problem. Who knows? He might find he just needs some seasoning to make that job more palatable.

Another powerful tool for the coachee who's stuck is the "just-do-it" or "act-as-if" approach. When a client told me that he didn't feel like an executive, despite recently having been promoted, I told him to start acting like one. Because of the behavioral theory of cognitive dissonance, when people start behaving in a certain way that's at odds with their beliefs, their beliefs tend to change. So, if a coachee feels stuck, ask him to behave as if he isn't stuck; his belief about the situation may follow suit.

Your Coachee Is Living with Regret

I've found two approaches that work here. The first is the get-over-it approach. When a person believes that the choice he has made is just the way it's going to be and there's no going back, he is more likely to move on. A person gets antsy when he thinks the door still might be open or that there's something he can do to get back to how things were before he made a particular choice. Help your coachee accept that he made the choice he did and that now he gets to move from where he is to where he wants to be.

The other approach is to help the coachee change his "What if . . . " conversation. Tell him this: "Instead of asking what in your life would be better *if only. . . ,* ask what might be worse. Really consider all that could have gone wrong had you made different choices."

Your Coachee Is Not Completing Assignments

Many of my coaching clients struggle when their own employees don't follow through on assignments. The first question I always ask them is "Did the employees help create them, or were these projects or tasks thrust upon them?" The thrusting may not have been overt. "Think hard," I say, "even if you got a 'yes' from the employee, did you make it impossible for her to say no?" The origin of the assignment is the same place to look when coachees aren't completing their assignments. Were the actions created by the coachee, created jointly, or imposed by the coach?

When your coachee doesn't complete assignments that he had a hand in inventing, you might try the following approaches:

◆ Point out the difference between what he accomplished and what he agreed to do. Sometimes the awareness that he will be held accountable and that you did notice the assignment wasn't completed is all it takes to get him to finish any future assignments.

◆ Find out what gremlins in his mind got in the way of his completing the action.

- Determine if the task needs to be changed.
- Break the assignment or task into smaller steps and check on these milestones more frequently than just during coaching conversations.
- Explore what he loses or misses by not completing the assignment (for example, "I don't get to feel in control without creating a budget") or what he gains by not doing it ("Ignorance is bliss; I can keep spending and just claim I didn't know how much I had."). Sometimes he'll discover that the pull not to do something actually is stronger than the pull to do it.
- Ask how he thinks he can get back on track.
- Express confidence that he can do what he sets out to do.

Your Coachee Pushes Away from Emotional Content

We talked in Step 2 about your shying away from emotional content and putting a lid on coaching, but how do you handle it when it's the coachee who's avoiding emotion? Like everything else, this can be a topic for coaching. Point out that as much as he wants to avoid how he's feeling, he'll keep carrying that feeling around with him until he does face it. Ask him to describe the benefits and risks of ignoring his emotions.

You can't force someone to "Feel!" on command. Your job as coach is simply to slow the coachee down when you hear a flicker of emotion and to call it to his attention, to ask him what he wants to do about it.

Sometimes you have to model emoting. You can do this honestly just by saying and showing how sad it makes you to watch him keep things bottled up inside.

Your Coachee Becomes Very Emotional

On the other end of the feelings spectrum is the coachee who is very free with his emotions. Often this comes in the form of tears, but other emotions also are common and relevant. With these coachees,

1. Acknowledge the coachee's emotion.
2. Describe the effect of his reaction on you and on the coaching session. Sometimes a strong emotion shown during a coaching session is an opportunity to address a wider issue. For instance, the coachee who gets extremely angry with you and who hears from his co-workers that he's an angry person has this opportunity for a supportive individual (you) to give him objective feedback on that emotion.
3. Determine if it's possible to continue.
4. Propose an approach for jointly refocusing on the issue you're trying to address.
5. Express support and reassurance.

Your Coachee Lacks Confidence or Is Fearful

This is one of the places where it's most fun to coach because the result of addressing a lack of confidence is having coachees who recognize that they're capable and strong. It's like watching someone meet themselves for the first time. It requires encouraging behavior on your part (this includes using the skill of acknowledging, covered in Step 6). Another really effective encouragement is pointing out the coachee's past and current accomplishments. With the underconfident coachee, you'll need to acknowledge even small accomplishments or those that might seem obvious. You'll need to make links between the actions he's performing on the job each day and those he's ultimately trying to do. Referring to his prior experience successfully doing something similar helps him see that he's capable of achieving future goals.

For instance, let's say your coachee wants to run a retreat for his staff, but he's afraid he won't be able to put together an agenda, stand up and deliver a program, find the proper venue, or get the staff to attend. If you know that he puts together agendas for

STEP 8

his boss each month, you may need to point out that this is a skill he already has. If he booked a social hall for his wife's birthday two years ago, he knows how to find a venue. If he tells you that, between coaching sessions, he mentioned the retreat idea to a staff member who seemed excited about it, you can congratulate him on taking a step toward getting the staff to attend. People who lack confidence often don't make the connection that what they're already doing is an aspect of what they want to be doing.

You'll also want to create a coaching environment in which the coachee's efforts are recognized, even if he doesn't achieve the desired results. Give him credit for trying his hardest, like your teachers did at school. Validate the coachee's current level of accomplishment while advocating greater achievement by reinforcing for him the importance of doing something he's not comfortable doing.

Rehearsing with your coachee is a common technique for overcoming a lack of confidence. Role-play tough conversations he needs to have with an employee, a boss, or a customer. Let him try out a presentation on you or give you some written report to read. When you role-play in the coaching session, your coachee learns that he has the words in him to say what needs to be said. He may never use them again, but if the situation arises where he must speak them, he has that extra level of assurance.

Encourage him to practice being confident. Have your coachee stand solidly with good posture and make eye contact with you. Then ask him to state aloud, in a good strong voice, something he's sure of. It can be something as basic as "My birthday is September sixth!" Ask him to notice what it feels like when he's totally confident. Have him mimic the same posture and voice and say something more risky, like, "I want to become a better manager." Work up to "I'm a terrific leader, and people want to be on my team" or "We can make $1 million more per year if we adapt this idea."

And teach him to rehearse mentally and to visualize the scary action going really well. Experiments with ballplayers have shown this mental imagery to be very real. One group of players practiced shooting baskets every day; another group simply closed their eyes and visualized shooting baskets (they thought about how they were standing, how it felt when the ball left their hands, how the ball arced into the basket). In subsequent games, the second group of players did as well as or better than the players who'd actually been shooting baskets.

Have your coachee speak with someone who has done what he's preparing to do, asking her how she did it. If you can find someone else who was nervous about doing it beforehand but did it anyway, that person would be an ideal role model for your coachee.

Your Coachee Is Overconfident

In our critical society, more people are taught to question their abilities and to be underconfident than to be overconfident. But in my coaching practice I have come across a couple of people who act or talk as if they're the greatest thing since sliced bread, even when their managers hired me to address their real performance problems.

First, determine whether the coachee really is blind to his inadequacies, or whether the bravado he displays actually is a cover-up for his lack of confidence. Sometimes, a straightforward "Do you really feel that way?" is all it takes to pull away his cover. Questions like "How else have you demonstrated this strength?" ask him either to support his assertions or to admit he doesn't really have certain abilities. Tell him how it sounds to you (or to his colleagues) when he talks that way. This coachee requires specific, timely observations. This is where coaches sometimes have to deliver the hard truth—the feedback that's probably going to come as a surprise or an embarrassment to the coachee. If you find that he's masking his self-doubt, you can move to the tips for handling a coachee who's underconfident.

But what if the coachee's overconfidence is a result of a blind spot in his awareness of himself as an employee, manager, partner, and the like? Have you seen the classic illustration of how to identify a blind spot? The Johari Window (figure 8.1) points to that sit-

STEP **8**

FIGURE 8.1

Johari Window

	OTHERS	
	Aware	**Unaware**
SELF **Aware**	*Obvious area of strength or development*	*A strength or shortfall that only you feel or experience; is it worth coaching?*
Unaware	*Blind spot; possible area for development*	*The unknown; buried so deeply it doesn't affect you*

uation in which your coachee is unaware of something about himself that is clear to others. Along the vertical axis of the figure is an assessment of how much a coachee is aware of a certain negative behavior or trait he exhibits; the horizontal axis shows how aware others are of that behavior or trait. If a negative characteristic falls into the quadrant where both he and others are aware of it, that's an obvious area for improvement. If, however, a negative characteristic or weakness falls into the quadrant where others are aware of it but he isn't, that's a blind spot for him. As his coach, you're there to help him see it. Similarly, a coach can help redirect a coachee who is focused on a negative trait or behavior that he's aware of but others aren't. Challenge him to figure out whether it's a fault that really needs correcting when he's the only one who knows about it. The final quadrant represents what's going on in the subconscious and wouldn't even surface as a coaching issue. Your job with a coachee who wishes to change negative behaviors or traits is to help him identify which quadrants his faults are in. When a troublesome characteristic is in that blind spot, help him see himself more clearly. (Incidentally, the Johari Window provides similar insight on positive traits that a person possesses. Again, the coach's role is to point out strengths the coachee has that he doesn't see in himself.)

Your Coachee Is Withdrawn

The typical tendency here is to try to pry the coachee out of his shell through questions. Another way to approach the withdrawn coachee is simply to let him be. You may have seen movies or read books in which therapists let their clients sit silently in their offices. Well, there's merit in doing that. The therapists are waiting for clients to get comfortable with them, waiting for clients to be ready to talk about what's on their minds, letting clients experience some silent time (and in the midst of a crazy, pressured workday, that silence might be productive all by itself). They also are acknowledging that the clients are in control of their therapy time, driving the process. I advocate trying this approach in your coaching sessions.

Eventually, the withdrawn coachee will begin to participate. When he does, your presenting a few good reflections of what you're hearing or seeing will go a long way. Much of what you're responding to as coach of a withdrawn individual is his nonverbal communication, so you might say, "I notice that your arms are crossed when we talk about that employee. What's that about?" or "I notice that your face gets red when I ask you certain types of questions and you don't have a response. What's going on for you?" or "I hear you saying 'no,'" but I wonder what you're leaving out of your response."

STEP **8**

When coaching becomes a drag, a bore, or a challenge for you or your coachee, it's a sign that something is happening that needs correction. Just dealing directly with whatever it is will increase your connection to your coachee, and that will result in new joy and energy in your interactions. Over time, you'll find yourself using some of the techniques from this step in the circumstances described here. You'll add your own situations and solutions as you address each unique snag in each unique coaching relationship you have. And you'll find that you, too, will get over some hurdles and become more confident in your own abilities to realign when things go bad.

Applying the Learning

◆ What signs are present to tell you whether your relationship is on or off track? How are each of your coaching relationships right now?

◆ How do you get yourself in the right frame of mind for coaching, especially when things between you and your coachee aren't at their best?

◆ What techniques for handling trouble spots do you want to remember now so that you can pull them out of your "toolkit" when things go bad?

◆ If you are experiencing any of the trouble spots described in the troubleshooting guide, try implementing some of the tips to address them.

NOTES

STEP NINE

Maintain Positive Changes

OVERVIEW

Determining readiness
for maintenance

Techniques for resisting
the "pull of the past"

Changes to the coaching
relationship during
maintenance

In Weight Watchers®, when a person reaches her goal weight, she moves from a regular membership to a lifetime membership designed to help her keep the weight off for the rest of her life. She usually attends meetings less frequently and only has to pay a fee when she rises above her goal weight. The continued weigh-ins and potential fees inform her when she gains just a pound or two so the gain doesn't go unchecked and turn into 20, 40, or 100 pounds and put her back where she started.

In coaching, there's a phase similar to a Weight Watchers lifetime membership. It starts when the coachee has made great progress, amassed many new tools, and doesn't want to lose sight of these positive changes over time. The coachee wants someone out there checking in with her periodically to help her maintain all of the growth she's achieved.

You'll know that you've reached this step when there isn't much new to talk about week after week; when all your coachee wants for herself is to remain in the productive, positive place where she is; or when she's consistently giving herself assignments and doing her own coaching using the tools and techniques you've helped her gather. It's almost as if she's coaching herself, with you as a witness or sounding board. And that's an apt description of who you might be as a coach at this step.

The questions in example 9.1 are one way for you and your coachee to determine if she's ready to move to the maintenance step. Those questions highlight quite a few conditions that would indicate the coachee is ready, including whether she recognizes accomplishments made through coaching, to whom she credits her success through coaching, and what tools she's acquired in the process. On all but statement 1, you would be looking for "I agree" responses from your coachee.

A person who is ready to move to maintenance realizes that she has put a lot of work into achieving the positive changes she's expe-

EXAMPLE 9.1

Is It Time for Maintenance?

Coachee instructions: Place a checkmark in the "I Agree" or "I Disagree" column to indicate your response to each of the six statements in the first column.

Statement	I Agree	I Disagree
1. I have achieved my goals because I worked with a great coach and had a good deal of support.		
2. I regularly use several of the tools I've learned in coaching.		
3. I know that I can continue to be successful.		
4. I clearly see the benefits of the changes I've made.		
5. I am more willing and able to take risks, take care of my needs, and try new things.		
6. I think differently about myself as an employee, leader, and human being since beginning coaching.		

Source: Full Experience Coaching.

riencing. She thanks herself for this and doesn't credit someone else, no matter how good a coach she had. Sure, a person needs a great support system, but someone ready to move to maintenance should be ready to take credit for making the changes she's made herself.

It's similarly important that the coach has observed the coachee selecting and using techniques to address her own situation. These techniques need not be complex or formal tools. (I think the word *tools* can intimidate people or raise their expectations unduly because they believe they'll find a magic solution in a model or exercise. Sometimes a technique can be as simple as standing up and stretching, or realizing you're in way over your head, or saying "no.") You'll recognize that the coachee is using these techniques when, week after week, she's sharing stories of how she resolved issues using perspectives or ideas you've talked about together. Make sure to congratulate her on her progress as you also consider whether it's time to move to a new step in coaching.

Many coachees reach this stage and become apprehensive instead of comfortable. They're afraid they can't continue to move ahead on their own. Without a coach, they fear their work lives will revert to how they used to be. That apprehension is a normal part of this phase, and even people who are apprehensive can embark on this step. Make the apprehension a coaching topic as you move forward.

As I mentioned previously, when a person sees the benefits of what she's doing, she's more likely to continue those activities. When she can articulate the feelings and results she's achieved through coaching and knows that she never wants to give those up, it's increasingly unlikely that she will. Questions 5 and 6 in example 9.1 ask whether she is doing or feeling things any differently than she did before. In those two questions, you may want to substitute other outcomes that relate more closely to what you two have been working on together.

Whether or not you use example 9.1 with your coachee, these are the types of considerations to take into account as you assess where you and your coachee are.

Overcoming the Pull of the Past

Maintenance can be a very rewarding step in coaching. Your coachee is now self-aware and self-directed. She's seen the changes that are possible for her and simply wants to make sure things don't start slipping back to how they were before the coaching process began.

But let's be realistic: The lure of the old and familiar is very strong. People have done things a certain way and interacted in the world a certain way for much of their lives. Even people who make significant changes during coaching can lose traction if unmonitored. Among the greatest challenges the coachee will face are the people in her life who display a strong negative reaction to change—even positive change. Why, they ask when a coachee becomes more protective of her time, schedules weekly check-in meetings with her employees, or goes back to school, must she upset the apple cart? Your coachee will appreciate your letting her know that this kind of reaction to her positive growth is normal.

Using the pull of the past as a topic for coaching, you'll want to discern whether the fear the coachee has about slipping back to how she once was has a real basis or is just imagined. If it's real, that makes it possible to take action, to make plans to avoid slippage. If there isn't actually a real force that might drag her back to the former status quo, then coaching now should concern implanting some positive self-talk that will help her remember there's nothing pulling her backward. A mantra like "I did this, I want what I've created here, and everything is working for me from this new place" should help keep her moving ahead.

Another technique for warding off the pull of the past is reminding your coachee—and having her ask others in her life to remind her—of all the times in the past when she said things like, "I'd feel so much better if . . ." or "I really want to do. . . ." Now that she's made the changes she always wanted to make, she may not be as aware of how she felt before she made them. A reminder from people who knew how much she was striving for what she's now achieved will provide another useful perspective for her to hold.

STEP **9**

Techniques for Sticking to It

The jury is out on how long it takes to break old habits or to form new ones. The best answers I can find say that it will depend on the person and what the habit is. People trying to give up bad habits should try to remember how long it took to form the habit in the first place. Something that may have taken years to develop isn't going to be eradicated simply or quickly. That said, there are certain actions the coachee can take to increase the likelihood that positive changes she's made during coaching will stick or that the negative routines she's eliminated won't creep back in. Two of these actions are celebrating and committing.

Celebrating connotes festivity and fun. Celebrations in coaching can be festive, or they can be more sober times of reflection on what your coachee has accomplished. Celebrating is allowing your coachee to experience the elation of achieving her goals, affirming the work she has put into reaching this step in the coaching process. The way you and she celebrate can range from a simple recitation of what she's accomplished to an elaborate "graduation" ceremony of her own creation. Or she can have a private celebration that consists simply of giving herself a reward—signing up for golf or tennis lessons, going out to lunch with a colleague or friend once a week, planning a vacation—that encourages her to continue being good to herself as she continues to act in and be a new way.

Reaching a milestone isn't the only opportunity to honor achievement. Celebrations and rewards can continue to motivate coachees and help them maintain the positive outcomes they've produced. Perhaps there's reason for celebration when a coachee has stuck with something for a given period of time, tried something new, or failed spectacularly (meaning her failure immediately was turned—by her—into a learning opportunity).

The time to have your coachee commit to maintaining the positive changes she's made through coaching is when she's excited about the results she's experienced in her work and personal life. At that moment, she's closely connected to how it feels to be more

STEP 9

effective and happy. It's this connection that will help her stick with whatever has worked for her.

The coaching questions that work well at this point include "What does committing to these changes mean to you?" "What will help you remain committed?" "What will be your signal that you're straying from this commitment?" and "What will you do when you notice that signal is present?"

You may want to have your coachee make her commitment more formal or public, from a simple statement made during a coaching session to a more elaborate commitment ceremony. During one of your discussions, ask her to make a declaration of what she is committed to and why. Her declaration might sound something like this: "I am committed to remaining present with my employees because I feel a whole new level of respect from them when I do so, and it really is the nicest part of my day." Or you might hold a ceremony during which she shares with you and others what she's gotten out of coaching. The more she can state aloud to others her intention to continue the growth she's achieved, the more likely that she will follow through on it. Request that she share her commitment to maintain the positive changes she's madewith at least six co-workers, family members, or friends. Like a wedding or life commitment ceremony, this public announcement also serves to call others to support her in her progress should she stray.

The maintenance phase involves more than merely sticking to the successes your coachee has achieved. In this step, the two of you also might establish new ways of tracking the results of coaching; you might want to work on locking in or broadening the learning achieved to this point; you might take this opportunity to deepen the coaching relationship the two of you have forged; or you might need to help your coachee find new supports in the workplace.

Tracking

My husband gave me an idea that I've gotten a lot of mileage out of in my coaching. The partner on a consulting team he managed had a new baby at home. The partner had to excuse himself from evening meetings to go home to his family. Everyone on the team was supportive and accepting of his need. The partner thought that the option should be extended to all team members. Why, he wondered, isn't there a widely accepted excuse for all of us—not just those with babies at home—to leave work on time, to avoid meetings at inconvenient times, or not to put in so many extra hours? My husband and his team invented the idea of having a "virtual baby." Each team member's baby was whatever was important to that person. Not only did each one have to name his or her virtual baby (Family Dinners Baby, Gym Workout Baby, and Favorite TV Program Baby were all part of the exercise); each person also committed a certain amount of time to the baby and kept track of how he or she honored that commitment. The team distributed graphs that tracked individual and team progress over time, and held each other accountable for sticking to the stated intention. So what is your coachee's virtual baby, and what sort of commitment is she willing to make to it? Is it taking regular guitar lessons? Spending two hours a week exploring other career options? Reading one business book a month? At regular intervals, have her report on how she's treating her commitment to her baby.

Another way to track is to extend the Weight Watchers model and think about what you want to have your coachee "weigh in" on periodically. Decide what's important to measure over time so that what you've covered in coaching remains alive, and check in on those indicators monthly or quarterly. For instance, ask your coachee, "How happy are you? How energetic? How motivated? How connected to your colleagues? How visible?" Just tracking these numbers over time—noticing trends and recommitting when numbers dip—is a powerful coaching tool.

Locking In the Learning

For years I taught listening and communication skills to a variety of audiences in diverse settings. My knowledge didn't always mean that in a stressful, emotional situation, I'd remember to use those skills. But I continued to be asked to deliver workshops on them

STEP **9**

and, over time, they did seep into my way of listening. At a minimum, I was constantly reminded of how important it is to listen actively. I always left those workshops recharged and recommitted to doing it.

You can create the same dynamic for your coachee by having her teach someone else what she's learned through coaching. She can lock in her learning by making a presentation at a staff meeting, writing an article for the company newsletter, outlining what she's learned for her team members, or serving as someone else's coach or adviser in the precise area about which she's learned so much.

Broadening the Learning

When my son was 8 years old, he said he could stop playing baseball because there was nothing more for him to learn. I explained to him that even the pros can still learn more about the game (and, although I didn't mention this to him, he was still far from a pro!). At this point in the coaching, ask your coachee to consider herself a pro, and then ask her what the pro in her area still needs to learn. If she's feeling satisfied with all aspects of her work and personal life, how would she describe feeling extraordinary?

Coaching often brings the coachee to some new understanding about herself or her work. When that understanding occurs is a good time to think about other areas of her life to which she can apply what she's learned. For instance, she may have learned to trust others so she could stop micromanaging—and she's gotten good at doing this. Now she can think about where else she might learn to trust others.

At this step, you may want to ask the coachee to take on a stretch assignment or challenge at work, or to step up to a new activity or responsibility. It's time to challenge her to do something that really tests her new skills or outlook. At this step, too, the coachee is ready to broaden her learning, to take on deeper and more expansive coaching assignments, like the legacy assignment in example 9.2.

EXAMPLE 9.2

Legacy Assignment

Coachee instructions: Read the paragraph below that describes what a legacy is and provides a framework for this assignment. Then review the guidelines for the mechanics of this assignment. Idea generators are provided at the end to help spark your creativity with this exercise.

> *A legacy is the gift you give to those who will follow you, what you bequeath to the next generation. To write a description of your legacy is to focus on the gifts you are leaving to your loved ones, your organization, and the world. This is not the same as writing your obituary—leaving a legacy doesn't mean you're dead. It's a dynamic process—something you can do every day, not merely at milestones.*

Guidelines

* The legacy assignment can take whatever form you desire—a newpaper article, a speech, a memo. Be as creative as you wish, and have fun!
* Don't be afraid to imagine what doesn't seem possible right now.
* Don't worry about offending anyone. For example, if you want your next position to be your boss's job, or even her boss's job, just say that. It isn't making any judgment on the boss or saying you expect her to get out of your way. You're simply describing a situation you see as a fit for you, the fulfillment of some of your dreams.
* Write in the past tense: Not "I hope I...," or "I want to...," but "I accomplished...," "I achieved...," "I did...." Put yourself temporarily in the future looking backward and describing things that already have happened.
* Write in the first person ("I did this or that") or in the third person ("In the last 10 years, Carl has...."). Some find the third person a bit easier because it feels more objective, less like bragging. The voice in which you write should fit the format you choose to use. For example, a speech you're delivering requires the first person, but the moderator's introduction of you before you deliver that speech requires the third person.

Idea Generators

* Imagine it's today's date in the year 2019 and you're returning to your current work unit, team, or organization for a visit. What have you been doing for the past 10 years? Where are you now in your life and career?
* Imagine you're leaving your current position (for a promotion, new job, retirement, or some other reason). What are you going on to do? What will you leave to your successor?
* Think of a milestone event you'll experience in life in the next 10 years—a major birthday, a job anniversary, the launch of a product or service you designed—and plan the speech you'll make at this celebration, recapping your successes and failures leading up to this event.
* What is the message you want to spread throughout the universe?

Source: Caryn Siegel and Sophie Oberstein, Redwood City Coaching Program.

STEP **9**

The coachee is ready to tackle broader questions, such as "What's my purpose in the world? What do I want to leave behind in this organization or in society? Just who do I want to be?" I've seen coachees write some really beautiful legacy descriptions that have inspired them in their current positions, new positions, and new roles in life.

Deepening the Coaching Relationship

The maintenance step isn't necessarily the end of the coaching relationship. In fact, sometimes it's quite the opposite—it's a chance to reevaluate the contribution that coaching is making and to redesign it so that it can be even more significant to both parties.

Relationship changes that are likely to occur during the maintenance step involve your current coaching schedule and the content of the sessions. If you've been meeting weekly for 45 minutes, consider whether this frequency and duration is still worthwhile. Also talk about the structure of the meetings you'll have going forward and discuss what role your coachee needs you to play at this step.

Who you are as a coach to your coachee can change at this step. For example, you both may decide to deepen your interactions by having you become more directly involved in her learning. Maybe you want to attend a workshop or read and discuss a business book together. Perhaps you have an opportunity to work with her on a project so that you can see her applying coaching concepts. That gives you an opening in your sessions to relate what she's doing on the project to the work you've done together. Or you might find yourself switching to monthly lunch meetings during which you're more often removing your coaching hat and replacing it with an adviser hat or colleague hat.

When relationship changes signify a real shift in the focus or format of your relationship, consider going through Step 10: Completing the Coaching Cycle. This will enable you to wrap up the old and begin anew. Completing Step 10 at this point doesn't mean you're marking the end of your relationship; rather, you're marking the end of a phase of that relationship.

Finally, although you should be soliciting feedback on your own coaching performance throughout prior steps, this step is one place where a more formal assessment might be administered. Because the way you're going to meet and interact as coach and coachee will be changing at this step, you have a perfect excuse (if you need one) to seek more formal input from your coachee. Example 9.3 is an evaluation you may wish to ask your coachee to complete. Use any or all of the items from this evaluation. Administer it verbally or in writing. Have the coachee complete it casually over the course of several sessions or do it in one fell swoop.

Finding New Supports

As you start to recede as a regular focal point in your coachee's support system, you'll want to help her connect with others who can be there for her on an ongoing basis. Some of these supports may already exist, and she may have to go out and establish connections with others. For example, regular meetings of professional associations may be good venues she can use to stay current in her field and expand her professional and personal network.

This is also a time to consider other coaching models that might be more sustainable than a one-on-one approach over the long term. These models might include monthly goal-setting teleconferences or group coaching. You'll find a unique coaching model at www.powerupcall.com, where individuals or small groups have an opportunity to share their intentions for each coming day and to celebrate the accomplishments of the day that just passed. And those are just a couple of the literally hundreds of coaching methods in existence.

If your coachee is interested in a different coaching model and can't find what she's looking for, it's a great assignment to have her

STEP 9

EXAMPLE 9.3

Coaching Evaluation

Coachee instructions: Respond honestly to the following questions about our coaching relationship for the full time we have been working together or for the time since you last completed an evaluation of my coaching.

1. What goals have you accomplished during the time we've worked together?

2. To what extent do you think coaching helped you achieve those goals? (100% = I couldn't have done this without a coach; 0% = coaching wasn't a factor in my getting where I am today): _____%
    Explanation:

3. What have you learned about yourself during the time we've worked together?

4. What can I do better as your coach?

5. Which exercises did you really enjoy/benefit from? Which didn't you get much out of?

6. What do you think are the three most important characteristics in a coach? Write one characteristic on each line and then circle a number that represents how I display that characteristic (1 = not at all; 5 = completely).

    _____   1   2   3   4   5

    _____   1   2   3   4   5

    _____   1   2   3   4   5

7. As your coach, have I done the following things? Circle "yes" or "no."

    a. Made appropriate time and space for you?   Yes   No
    b. Built trust and maintained confidentiality?   Yes   No
    c. Given you constructive feedback?   Yes   No
    d. Been open and flexible?   Yes   No
    e. Established accountability?   Yes   No
    f. Kept the focus on you and your development?   Yes   No

8. If you would refer me to someone else as a coach, what would you tell others are my strengths?

Source: Full Experience Coaching.

create her own model. For instance, one of my clients created a support group in her workplace for employees who were completing degree programs during their nonwork hours. Group members brainstormed strategies for getting it all done, reviewed each other's school work, and threw graduation parties to celebrate one another's successes. Another client created monthly executive roundtable breakfast meetings for senior managers in his industry. These meetings addressed the question "What keeps you up at night?" and participants brainstormed solutions together.

Maintenance is about having your coachee continue to do the things that have worked for her in coaching thus far, and continue feeling good about doing them. This step is intended to make new work habits stick. Sure, there'll be days when she gets discouraged or forgets everything she learned through coaching. And if you help her discover her most effective techniques for remembering her commitment to the positive strides she's made, those days will become less troublesome and less frequent.

Applying the Learning

> POINTER
>
> The toughest thing about success is that you've got to keep on being a success. – *Irving Berlin, composer*

- ◆ How have you maintained positive changes you've made in your life? How can you use your experience to help your coachee maintain her changes?
- ◆ What is the legacy you want to leave as a coach, an employee, a person? Complete example 9.2 to describe your own legacy.
- ◆ Ask your coachee to complete example 9.1 to determine whether she's ready to move to the maintenance step. If so, look over the ideas in this step together to decide how you both want to proceed.

STEP **9**

STEP **9**

Complete the Coaching Cycle

I sense a longing in our society: People like to accomplish things; they like to take a project from start to finish successfully. There's a desire to stand at the end of a process and to feel complete. For many people, however, the real opportunity to finish something ended with college—with its essay deadlines, test dates, and semester endings.

It isn't that we aren't finishing things anymore, but we're often just too busy to realize that we've actually achieved a desired result or reached the end of an activity or process. Often we're swept up in year-round goings-on and don't have natural breaks that tell us to slow down and notice what's ending and what's now possible.

I notice that when my clients are nearing the end of one project, relationship, or job, they move so quickly into the next one that they don't give themselves credit for what they've just completed. They don't even take time to contemplate what the experience has taught them, what might be valuable for them to take along to the next endeavor. When we don't take time for closure, we continue to carry with us parts of what's now in the past. That

STEP **10**

Don't let yesterday take up too much of today.

– Will Rogers, humorist

consumes energy that we need for what's going to happen next in our lives.

Because coaching is a relationship designed from the beginning to end eventually (because coaching is meant to create independence and to encourage individuals to achieve their own fulfillment), it's a ripe opportunity for exploring and modeling this concept of ending. This is true whether you've established a formal coaching relationship with an employee or you're going separate ways after a relationship with someone you've been close to. Completion can come at the end of the coaching relationship or at certain milestones along the way.

Although lots of energy and thought go into the earlier coaching steps, there is relatively little preparation for the crucial end phase of the process. This step can provide a great opportunity for growth and reflection, whether a relationship has been positive or negative. Not giving this step in the coaching cycle your attention would be like creating a fabulous PowerPoint presentation, turning it on for your audience, and walking away.

What Does It Mean to Complete the Coaching Cycle?

In this society of rapid movement, what is it to end things properly? Is closure even possible? As I'm sure you're used to by now, there isn't a right answer here. But there are some questions that you might want to consider yourself—and to discuss with your coachee—as you reach Step 10.

◆ **What is closure to you?** With your coachee, define closure. You might want to use some of the same techniques you used to define coaching in Step 1 or just talk about what completing something means to each of you.

◆ **Can you describe closure with a metaphor?** Is it wrapping up a present with a tidy bow, breaking through a finish line, or tucking a child into bed at night? Using a metaphor will help you visualize what you're trying to do, the feeling you're trying to create, when you start this process with your coachee.

◆ **What feelings are associated with closure for you?** Is there generally fear as something familiar comes to an end, or exhilaration at being able to start something new? Does closure feel warm and safe to you, or vast and unattainable?

When Is It Time to Complete the Cycle?

Knowing when a coaching relationship needs to conclude is a very tricky skill. The signs you think indicate that the relationship might be heading for an end often are really a coachee's resistance to the work you're doing, and coaching at that time may be more important than ever before. For instance, when a coachee seems to be less engaged in the process, it could mean that he's simply achieved what he needed to and is ready to branch out on his own; or it may mean that he's resistant to or threatened by an assignment and needs to be pushed to identify what's going on and to get past it to some breakthrough. Similarly, a coachee may want to use outside issues, such as an increased workload or personal pressures like a loved one's illness or a divorce, to justify ending the coaching process, but he actually may need the structure, support, or accountability that coaching provides during those difficult times.

Generally, you must use your intuition to reveal issues you feel are present that may indicate that coaching has served its purpose, and then check with your coachee to see if he feels the same way. Check out your perceptions and assumptions when the first indicators appear. Also be aware that what you think you see may be a reflection of your own anxiety, fear, or hope.

When I was starting out as a coach, I had a client I thought I wasn't serving well. I went so far as to ask other coaches I thought might be better matches if they'd be interested in working with him. But when I raised the issue with him, he said he thought our differences in approaching his situation had been very useful and challenged him to think in new ways. He wanted to continue working with me.

Here are some signs that a coaching relationship may be ready to end:

◆ You've spent far too many sessions doing clean-up work or troubleshooting and, despite repeated efforts to realign, you both agree it's not working.

◆ You've been in the maintenance step for so long that you're no longer coaching; for example, you're sharing your issues with the coachee, there are no more assignments, or it feels more like two colleagues getting together to chat.

◆ You've come to the end of an agreed timeframe or the end of a formal coaching program.

◆ You no longer can give coaching the time or energy needed.

◆ The logistics no longer work. For example, your coachee wants coaching after work hours and you can only be there for him during the workday, or he moves to another facility or state and your coaching is done face-to-face rather than on the phone.

◆ You become friends and drift into a more informal relationship based on the growing familiarity between you. Friends don't make good coaches because they're invested in the relationship in a different way and often have individual agendas. They may also hold back constructive feedback in fear of jeopardizing the friendship.

◆ It's just not a good fit between the two of you. The coachee has a need for a coach with a different style or approach. Something about the chemistry between you, or your differing styles and approaches, simply may mean it isn't a good match.

◆ The energy that either or both of you used to get from the coaching sessions is not as long-lasting as it used to be.

What Keeps Us from Ending Properly?

Despite the presence of one or more of those signs, coach and coachee often hang on indefinitely or may be surprised when the relationship ends earlier than either individual anticipated. Let's look at the latter situation first. What goes wrong and leaves one or both people surprised by the abruptness of the end? I'd say this kind of improper ending most often results from a lack of communication. In a completely open coaching relationship, there aren't many surprises. You each know how the other person feels about you and the work you're doing. It's analogous to a good performance review. If you've communicated with your employee throughout the year and he knows how he's doing, that review doesn't come as a shock to him. Being surprised also shows you haven't talked from the beginning about how and when to end coaching.

Even if you have talked about it, don't make any assumptions. I had two clients who'd worked with me for a long time and made great strides. I thought, with all they'd accomplished, they were ready to end. We'd talked about it from the beginning. So I started talking and planning completion with them, without asking if they were ready. They really were taken aback. They hadn't realized we'd be ending just yet and weren't prepared for that conversation.

Some things that keep us too long in coaching relationships include the following:

- ◆ **Inertia**—One or both of you believe it's easier to let the relationship disintegrate or fizzle out than to address the ending directly.
- ◆ **Comfort**—Who doesn't want someone who will focus on and listen to him or her? What a nice routine it is to talk regularly and be helped to steer your ship. The problem is that hiding in this comfort is dependence.
- ◆ **Desire not to offend**—The coachee doesn't want to hurt the coach's feelings and hangs on for that reason alone. This is especially likely when the coach is one's boss or

STEP 10

someone who might help him in his future career. Coachees often feel indebted to their coaches for all that the coaches have done for them; they feel a sense of obligation that means they wouldn't suggest ending.

◆ **Difficulty dealing with closure**—Some individuals have difficulty with relationship endings. This is particularly problematic when neither party knows how to let go or when both have limited experience with endings.

◆ **Fear or anxiety about change**—Worry about what will happen when a relationship ends makes lack of closure the preferred situation.

◆ **Feeling that ending is admitting to failure**—If we stop the coaching, am I saying that coaching doesn't work? Am I admitting that I'm a bad coachee (or a bad coach)? One client told me that several managers in his organization had started a coaching program together. Their relationships were all going great, but his wasn't. He thought something had to be wrong with him when his coaching pair fell apart and their pairs didn't. A coach may feel she's failed to "cure" her coachee and that she hasn't done her job.

◆ **Striving for perfection**—As much as we prepare for ending well, please understand that you can never tie up all the loose ends of life. Rarely is closure clean and straightforward. Don't beat yourself up if you have to complete the cycle in a sloppy, inelegant way. Don't worry if not everything your coachee set out to achieve has been accomplished. Sometimes a coachee needs a period of time for the coaching to sink in, for the economy to change in a way that will accommodate his goals, for the right person to cross his path, or for the right level of experience and maturity to develop, before an issue actually can be resolved. Months after we've stopped working together, I hear from clients who are only then realizing the results of our coaching conversations.

How Do You End a Coaching Relationship?

There are four parts to a good ending. These are

1. **noticing a sign in the coaching relationship**—recognizing that something is changing in the relationship and that you both might be better served by ending the relationship (at least in its current form)

2. **learning**—incorporating into your trove of life lessons your successes and failures over the period in which you worked together

3. **celebrating**—acknowledging what you've each contributed to the relationship and to the outcomes you've experienced together; letting yourself have some fun to recognize this contribution

4. **intention setting**—being clear and purposeful about what comes next and how you want to approach that next situation.

Noticing the Signs

So you notice some of the signs described above. How do you know if the relationship would be better served if you parted ways? Here's how a conversation about ending the process might sound:

> ***Coach:*** Jane, can we take a moment today to talk about where our relationship is since you were promoted last month?
>
> ***Coachee:*** Sure.
>
> ***Coach:*** Great. I've noticed that, since your promotion, there hasn't been the same energy in our interactions and, more often than before, your assignments aren't completed. What have you noticed?
>
> ***Coachee:*** Well, yeah. I guess I noticed the energy's been a little lower. You know that promotion was a big thing and it's over, and I've been really busy trying to put things in

order in my department since becoming the boss. I just don't have the same kind of time.

Coach: That makes sense. You're in a new place and have new concerns and challenges. Are you interested in seeing how coaching can help you in this transition period?

Coachee: Oh, yeah. I need your advice more than ever now.

Coach: That sounds like something different than you needed from me before. What do you need from me as a coach right now?

Coachee: Well, I'd love some more specific suggestions of how to hit the ground running without burning out.

Such a conversation may be needed not just once but a few times until you settle on what you each need from the other and whether you can provide it. The fundamental questions to ask at this stage are

◆ Are you still interested?
◆ Are we making progress?
◆ I've noticed. . . . What have you noticed?
◆ How can I help you right now?

These conversations often will lead to recontracting rather than ending. That's OK. Coaching results appear over time, and cycles of movement and stagnation are normal. It's important for the coach always to keep a finger on the pulse of the relationship itself. There are three entities in the coaching process—the coachee, the coach, and their relationship. The needs of all three entities must be identified and addressed. And it's the coach who needs to say what is most difficult to say: "This relationship may have run its course. What do you think?"

Be careful here to make it clear that you enjoy working with your coachee and aren't "firing" him; that you aren't thinking of stopping your work together because he's hopeless or because he didn't follow through on some assignment. Explain that you're raising the issue because you've seen some signs that the relationship itself isn't working or has served its purpose. It's important to let the coachee know two things: (1) Ending a relationship is natural and OK, and (2) you neither need nor want to end this one unilaterally. Many coaching pairs adopt the "no-fault rule" at the start of their relationship; this rule holds that there is no blaming if the partnership is not working or if one person is uncomfortable with it.

If your noticing-signs conversations do lead to an ending, there are options to be discussed: Will you stop completely within the next several weeks and transition back to your former relationship as colleagues or boss/employee? Will you meet less and less frequently, weaning off slowly? Or will you recontract for another period of time and design a new coaching relationship for that period?

If you choose to end the relationship after a few more sessions, explicitly discuss how it will feel to return to your former relationship. Keep some of your coaching agreements—like confidentiality—in place indefinitely. Assure the coachee that nothing he has said will show up in his performance evaluations or will surface during a meeting. Make sure you both talk about what it will take to be comfortable again in your former roles.

Weaning off of coaching more slowly is simply that. It's considering all of the questions and ideas in this step, just over a longer period of time. It might mean there is still a coaching project or assignment the coachee is completing at the same time that you two are focused on ending activities. What you provide during this period is observation of how well the coachee is doing on his own, integrating the skills he's honed during coaching. Usually the people who elect to wean off more slowly lack some confidence that they can maintain the changes they've made through coaching without regular contact, so pointing out what he's doing well is extremely beneficial in fostering ongoing independence.

Recontracting happens frequently during a dynamic and collaborative coaching relationship. What's different here is that now you may want to begin implementing some sort of completion exercises at each transition point in your relationship—for example, when you're about to move from meeting every other week to meeting once a month, when you're going to change the focus of your coaching from getting a promotion to managing "difficult" employees in the coachee's new role, or even when your coachee is asking simply for a different kind of feedback from you or you're asking him to recommit to following through on assignments. In any of those situations, some of the noticing, learning, celebration, and intention-setting activities and questions from this step can be valuable additions.

Learning from the Successes and Failures

How many times have you left a conference or workshop eager to put into practice the great things you've learned—but found that demands at work or home got in the way or that you simply forgot some of the details before you had a chance to put them to use? Taking time to process what you've learned at these workshops increases the likelihood that you'll incorporate at least some of it into your day-to-day work. The same is true with coaching. If the lessons learned are going to stick, you and your coachee really need to sit down and sort them out. Identify the lessons that are worth carrying beyond the coaching. Tool 10.1 suggests some activities to pursue with your coachee at the point of completion. They will prompt a conscious review of the exercises done, discoveries made, and lessons learned in coaching.

Celebrating Contributions and Outcomes

Leaders whom team members respect take time to celebrate when projects are completed. They understand that celebrating garners good will, shows real appreciation for the efforts of a hard-working team, motivates team members to continue their good performance, and builds relationships and rapport. Celebrations include team outings, gifts, awards, luncheons, and so forth. All of those also are appropriate ways to celebrate the work you and your coachee have done together. As you celebrate, encourage the coachee to acknowledge himself and you as his coach. You can celebrate even if the relationship wasn't what you would deem an unmitigated success.

TOOL 10.1

Completion Activities

1. Pose powerful questions like these:
   * What are you taking away from this experience?
   * What have been your key discoveries?
   * Looking back on where we've been together, what has worked? What hasn't?
   * What shifts did you experience?

2. Have the coachee write the story of where he's been—who he was when you started and who he is now.

3. Have the coachee create a collage, poster, mindmap, or other graphic that summarizes what was most important to him during the process.

4. Either have the coachee create a journal of his coaching experience—or you can create it for him. The journals my clients create include quotes and ideas that had meaning for them, names and pictures of their gremlins, their values, their life purpose statements, and so forth. Even when I create a journal for a client (as a parting gift), I first talk with my client about what I'm planning to include. Doing so becomes a useful activity because it requires him to reflect on what's been most meaningful for him throughout coaching. I also include reminders of how he can use each bit of helpful information in the journal. For instance, if we've done a lot of work together on changing perspective, I might include a section of tips that remind him to continue seeking new perspectives for circumstances that are challenging (see example 10.1). One of the purposes of the journal is to remind the coachee of the exercises completed during coaching sessions and the examples and tools used.

Celebrate the coachee's having put aside other pressing concerns to take part in the coaching sessions, celebrate his honesty, or even that he tried and failed. Here are several suggestions for coaching-end celebrations:

   ◆ Give your coachee a fun gift. My clients receive Juicy Living Cards (Sark's painted cards with positive messages; Hay House, 2003), Dr. Seuss's *Oh, the Places You'll Go!* (Random House, 1993), music I think they'll like, or posters with affirming ideas printed on them.

   ◆ Go out and have a celebratory drink with your coachee.

   ◆ Ask "What do you need to say to be complete?" At the Coaches Training Institute where I took my coaching

EXAMPLE 10.1

Sample Page from a Completion Journal

Tips for Changing Your Perspective

* If you're feeling stuck, consider whether you're holding on too tightly to a limiting perspective. What "shoulds" are present in this situation?

* Ask yourself "Is this perspective true?"

* What other perspectives on this situation are there? (How are you looking at it? What's another point of view? What's another? And then another?)

* Don't be afraid to look at your situation from some "out-there"/wacky/unrelated perspectives. Set aside your current view and brainstorm a list of random elements related to a completely different topic. Look at that list and consider how any item there could apply to your current situation.

* Determine which perspective you choose to hold in this situation. What aspect(s) of the situation might be different when viewed from that new perspective?

* Explore this question: "Where else in your life can you use this perspective?"

Source: Full Experience Coaching.

courses, every session ended with time for "completion"—the opportunity to say what you needed to say to be complete in the moment. It wasn't necessarily all you had to say on the topic, and you always could choose to say nothing. It's the simplest way to wrap up a meeting, a phone call, a training program, a session, or a relationship; and it helps people transition back to their typical activities. Noting that this idea is listed under celebrating rather than learning makes the point that you're not asking coachees to spit back whatever they've picked up as a learning; it's letting them describe any reactions they had, express any thank-yous they want to give, offer any recognition, or share any feelings.

Celebrating isn't just a feel-good perk. It's an important management and coaching tool.

Intention Setting

Setting intentions in your last session together can be rather bitter-sweet. You know that you won't be checking in with your coachee anymore to see what progress he's made on his intentions, but you're thrilled that he's equipped to go ahead and make progress on his own. Here are some ways to create and establish accountability around intentions that you won't be part of bringing to fruition:

- Ask "Where are you going? What's next? What do you hope for?"
- Discuss what support your coachee will need in pursuing those plans.
- Put your coachee's significant future dates in your calendar and contact him on those dates. For instance, if he has a big meeting in two months or if a project he's been work-ing on is coming to fruition in the next quarter, create a tickler in your calendar to check in with him before or after that event.
- Because he'll no longer regularly be reporting to you on the progress of his goals, have him create in his calendar some artificial deadlines by which time he wants to have made certain progress. Rather than you checking on him on those dates, he'll have a reminder to monitor his own growth and acquisition of goals.
- The final sessions should include a revisiting of the base-line measures that you first recorded when you were creat-ing goals back in Step 5. How have the meaningful meas-urements changed over time during coaching? How much more confident/alive/efficient has he become? How can he integrate the indicators into his life going forward?
- Discuss tools and strategies he'll use when future times get tough. List resources he can go to when he gets stuck in certain areas.

Noticing, learning, celebrating, and intention setting all can happen in one meeting or over several sessions. Sometimes the four parts of completing the coaching cycle are distinguished from each other. That is, you really have a distinct celebration of what the coachee has accomplished and there is no recap of learning or intention setting at all. Or maybe you have a session devoted strictly to next steps. That's an entirely valid way to go. Sometimes these four things overlap, and you find yourself bouncing from celebrating to intention setting to celebrating. That's equally valid. And completion may not happen during the meetings at all. Much like the work of coaching, it can happen between or after sessions. Leave the door open for your coachee to come back to you after your final meeting to share what he couldn't share at the time.

As at every other step, some coaches prefer to document completion using a written form. Examples 10.2 and 10.3 show two different approaches to that completion form. Example 10.2 is the form I use with my clients, and it comprises five open-ended questions—two on learning, two on celebrating, and one on intention setting. Example 10.3 is adapted from the work of coach Ben Dooley. It has several more questions, and each one is categorized by which aspect of completion is being covered.

The Coach's Completion

Like other people in our rushed society, you as a coach may fail to mark the end of one coaching relationship by just moving directly into another. But you have much to learn from each coaching relationship you complete, and drawing a thoughtful close to a relationship will help you continue to be engaged and excited about yourself and your coaching. You need to complete as much as your coachees do.

Just as you had the coachee revisit his baseline measures, this is an ideal time to do a post-coaching assessment of your skills. Go

EXAMPLE 10.2

Brief Coaching Completion Form

Coachee instructions: Thank you for being my client. And thank you for recognizing it was time for you to move on, and for making that known. Below are some questions to help us focus our remaining sessions together. Please take some time to think about your answers. If you want to write your responses (and send them to me) before we talk again, that's great. It's just as great if you'd prefer simply to look them over now and bring your thoughts to our next session.

1.   What has changed for you as a result of coaching?

2.   What do you want to remember about this coaching? (For example, what were some themes you discovered in our work together? What exercises did you particularly like? What "a-ha!" moments did you have?)

3.   How do you want to acknowledge yourself and what you've contributed to the coaching process?

4.   What is it that you have to say to feel complete (achieve closure) concerning any trouble spots we experienced together?

5.   How should our relationship continue when your coaching is complete?

STEP 10

Source: Full Experience Coaching.

EXAMPLE 10.3

In-Depth Completion Form

Coachee instructions: All events and relationships have a natural arc, a beginning, middle, and end (and there are no rules for how long each phase must be). Now the arc of our coaching relationship is reaching its end. Completion of coaching means that you've grown, shifted, and changed so that the current structure of this relationship isn't serving you as it once did. You're ready for something new to enter your life, and the best way to approach it is to allow some time to reflect on what has happened during the coaching process. Reflect with an appreciative eye rather than with judgment or blame.

Please take some time between now and our final session to consider the questions below. There are no right or wrong answers, and none of your responses will be "letting me (or anyone else) down." These questions will focus your thoughts and intentions. They'll help you honor and celebrate the journey you've taken, acknowledge your successes and failures, and clearly identify where you are *right now*. Doing all of those things will enable you to remain connected to your values and passions and continue to make power-ful, effective advancements toward your goals.

At our final meeting, you'll have a chance to share all you've discovered and to say whatever you need to say to feel complete. Until then, I look forward to celebrating you stepping into a new phase of your life.

---

1. Where is the biggest area of your life/work in which you've grown?

---

2. How can you keep that growth alive for yourself?

---

3. How else have you changed (in relationships, personal growth, work, health, and so forth)?

---

4. Of what are you most proud?

---

5. What did you find most scary during the coaching?

---

6. For what do you forgive yourself?

Next Steps

---

1. What's next for you?

---

2. What new obstacles are in the way?

3. In what area do you wish to grow more?

4. How will you stay connected to and focused on your ongoing growth?

Our Coaching Experience

1. What has worked in our coaching time together?

2. What has not worked or what would you like to have seen more of in our sessions?

Options for Continued Maintenance

As you go forward with this new awareness and appreciation of your values, skills, vision, and goals, it may be beneficial to continue working with a coach in a new structure. Here are some options for you to consider:

* Hire a new coach who will work with you on specific new needs and direction.
* Find a new coach for general work. Coaches offer different styles and approaches and can have completely different effects on your growth and learning.
* Continue our work on a check-in basis, either once a month or every two or three months.
* Create a solid noncoaching support structure in your own circle to help keep you focused and accountable.

Celebration

How do you want to celebrate and honor yourself in this ending? For example, do you want to write a letter to yourself, have a glass of wine with your coach, take a walk and reflect on your transition, share your results with your boss, treat yourself to something special?

STEP 10

Source: Adapted from the work of Ben Dooley and used with permission.

back to worksheet 1.1 and see how your answers have changed. Or, consider the following questions:

◆ What has this coachee taught me?

◆ How have I changed as a coach?

◆ Is there something I haven't said to my coachee?

Create a process and ritual for closing out a coaching relationship. This can be something very basic, like taking a deep breath and bringing to mind a picture of the person with whom you're finishing the coaching cycle. Then write a quick note or journal entry about your experience working with him and what it taught you.

Whether closure is unanticipated or planned, dealing with it together and directly is critical for a successful coaching relationship. It is during the closure conversation that learning is cemented, that appreciation is articulated, and that celebration occurs. It is also the occasion for considering whether this relationship should continue and, if so, on what basis.

When we don't come to closure, we dissipate our energy for future projects by continuing to carry the past with us, and we miss the peace of successful completion.

> **POINTER**
>
> Great is the art of beginning, but greater is the art of ending. – *Lazarus Long, fictional character featured in a number of science fiction novels by Robert A. Heinlein*

Applying the Learning

◆ Is your coaching relationship showing any signs that it might be time to recontract or complete?

◆ Are you continuing this coaching relationship because of inertia, comfort, fear of offending your coachee, or any of the other unconstructive reasons discussed in this step?

◆ What do you want your completion process to include for you and your coachee?

◆ What are some 10-minute, 30-minute, 60-minute, and half-day activities you can do to celebrate when you and your coachee reach certain milestones or finish a phase of your coaching relationship?

NOTES

STEP 10

10

CONCLUSION

I use the CTI model to end all of the workshops I facilitate, giving each participant a chance to say whatever it is he or she needs to say to process the information he or she has taken in and to acknowledge what has happened over the period we've been working together. During one of these circles recently, a participant who'd been rather quiet all day said, "I enjoyed the workshop, and I especially want to thank you for simply asking during one of today's exercises, 'What is your dream?' No one has asked me that in more years than I can remember. I am so thankful to have gotten back in touch with my dream today."

Like I did for this program participant, you're about to go into the workplace and ask powerful questions that people haven't been asked in a long time. You're about to touch people in ways that will inspire them and make them feel good about themselves. The people you're going to coach in your workplace are so lucky to have you in their lives; your organizations are lucky to have you. Congratulations on embarking on this journey.

After countless completion circles like the one at the end of that workshop, and through my experience coaching others, I've now heard a lot of comments about what people get out of coaching. Those learnings fall into several categories that I thought I'd share with you because you're going to come across them in your coaching, too. These are concepts that can guide you in your coaching because they cover universal truths about how people make positive changes and achieve greatness in their lives.

◆ **Getting comfortable with "right now" is key.** When we realize that the decisions we're making today don't have to last our whole lives, there's a lot less pressure to make the right ones. When we look from a right-now perspective at a situation we're in that might not be perfect for the long term, we often see that it's pretty darn good as it is. We may not want the situation to continue unchanged forever, but if we look at how it's working for us in this moment, we may find peace with it.

I know this was true for me when I started my coaching practice. At first, I woke each morning panicking that I didn't have enough clients. But then I took a hard look at what having fewer clients was allowing me—I was able to be with my two young children more often and in less stressful circumstances. I even made it to the gym a couple of days a week. Even more important, I realized that clients were coming; that when one client was winding down, another was showing up. I saw that the lifestyle I was leading and the work I was doing were perfect for where I was at that moment. Someday, I thought, I might want to have more clients at a time, make more money as a coach, or even write a book (!), and I didn't have to toss that dream aside. I just had to know that the practice I'd built was just right for the given moment in time. I let go of that constant anxiety and really enjoyed the small coaching practice I already had.

◆ **Playing to our strengths produces rapid growth and movement.** In Step 3, I shared a premise from the book *Good to Great*. I was talking about in whom to invest your coaching resources. The same concept can be applied to what your coachee decides to work on in coaching. When we capitalize on those things that make us great, we become exceptional; people are attracted to us, and we can transform our dreams into reality. If we focus instead on those parts of us that are mediocre and need fixing, we'll take longer, grow discouraged, and not get as far.

This isn't to say that we can ignore those areas in us that need work. We need some level of competence in areas where we don't excel. For instance, if following up or filling out forms is an area of weakness, you can't just stop calling people back or stop completing your time card. You have to develop a minimum level of ability in any area that can't be erased from your life.

But when we share our special beauty and wisdom— our unique strengths—with the world, that's when we shine. Investing our energies for self-improvement and growth in the areas in which we excel will yield the greatest and most fulfilling returns. (Incidentally, when we rise to the greatness within us, and are engaged in the world at that level, we can find someone else whose strength is in one of our weak areas. In the example above, that would mean finding someone who is great at and enjoys handling our calls or completing our paperwork.)

Identifying our strengths also may point the way to work that suits us better than what we are doing currently. One of my clients received several annual performance reviews that cited her written communication and computer skills as needing improvement. Those negative comments got much more of her attention than did the good-to-glowing comments elsewhere in the evaluation. She struggled through training courses in these areas of weakness, but the concepts never stuck with her. When we started working together, I asked her to tell me about the strengths cited in her reviews: wonderful people-person, the one customers waited to talk to, the one who brought harmony to departmental meetings, the person who welcomed and trained new employees in the division. We changed her focus from trying to overcome her weaknesses to sharing her strengths more purposefully and visibly. She ended up moving to a training department and excelling as a standup trainer. She played to her strengths.

Many people are simply not aware that their strengths truly are strengths. They just take them as givens and assume that the traits and talents that come naturally to them are equally natural for everyone. Perhaps they don't realize that their common sense isn't always that common.

They don't appreciate that what they're bringing to the table is unique and needed. Altering this lack of awareness is an aspect of coaching that I love. It feels great to help a coachee see that what he or she takes as normal and not extraordinary is really unusual and fantastic.

◆ **We won't get what we want if we don't know what it is.** One evening, we hosted in our home a welcome reception for our temple's new rabbi. A half-hour before the reception began, my husband came home from work and began worrying aloud (that's a generous way of saying he started second-guessing me). "Will that be enough food? Are these plates too small? Where's the wine?" Feeling criticized, I reacted angrily and defensively: "I've got this all under control," I snapped. "And why are you just getting interested in this party now?" Everything escalated until, in exasperation, he asked, "What do you want from me?" I stopped. I thought about this commonly voiced question and answered, "I want you to say something nice about what I've done here." And he did. He said, "Well, I can't believe you pulled this party together after your whole day at work, and I thank you for always welcoming people into our house and keeping it ready for them." Just what I needed. (And, by the way, there was plenty of food.) Why this story? Because all it took in that situation was my stopping to think of what I wanted and asking for it. Had I done that earlier, perhaps we could have avoided the bigger argument. This is the question the workshop leaders in my coach training taught me to ask when all other coaching questions failed: What do you want?

Knowing what you want is more than being able to ask for something tangible and getting it, as in that story; it demands first that you know the objective of your communication or the outcome you want for a situation. Recently, a friend was talking to me about an argument she'd been having with her boss. She talked about wanting to write a letter to explain her side of the story. "That's nice," I said, "but what do you want him to do as a result of reading it—agree with you? That might not be realistic. Repair your relationship? If so, do you need to explain your side (again)? Perhaps it would be better to write the following in a letter: "I want to have a good working relationship with you, as we once had. I want to sit down and talk about what we each can do to recreate that."

You also must know that what you're asking for is really what you want. I have clients who say they want to find a new job, but really just want their current job to be more engaging. Some clients say they want higher positions in their organizations—and even start applying for them—when they actually doubt that they could do the new job and are only applying because they think they're *supposed* to want to advance in the organization. I had a client who mourned the demise of a business plan she'd created. But when I asked her if she truly would have wanted to devote the next phase of her career to that business, she realized it wouldn't have been a fit with her strengths and it would have become a burden.

Many of my clients don't achieve the goals they initially contact me about—and I'm proud of that. Instead, almost all of them tell me they live their day-to-day lives more happily and more aware; they live more purposefully each day. Many of them come to realize that the things they initially thought they wanted weren't actually what they wanted (only what had been expected of them), or that they really hadn't thought through what they wanted and were only reacting to circumstances.

◆ **Possibilities open when you separate yourself from your circumstances.** A common lament I hear from my clients sounds like this: "I never used to be the type of person who was insolent with my boss" or "I'm not a person who forgets things, so why did I miss that meeting?" I tell them, "You may not be the type of person who is insolent with your boss (or who forgets things, or who's a quitter, or who needs recognition); you're just in circumstances that are making you act that way. You can change the circumstances without changing who you are." A person's circumstances can change and her or his reaction to those circumstances can be uncharacteristic without changing the person.

Not getting a particular promotion doesn't mean you're not promotable. Giving up a particular dream doesn't mean you'll never amount to anything. So many clients agonize unnecessarily over situations they're in because they're not seeing them simply as *situations they're in*. Rather, they confuse the transitory circumstances with their intrinsic identities and give entirely too much weight to the situation.

For example, a client was getting negative feedback on a project he was managing. It led him to remark that he wasn't a good manager and to refrain from applying for a management position that was open in his department. True, there were things that he could have been doing better as project manager, but the project was set up to fail. Rather than seeing himself embroiled in a bad project, he took his experience to mean he wasn't capable of managing well. Those are two separate issues, and they need to be viewed separately and realistically.

◆ **When we put some positive energy into the world, we experience positive results.** My mother always says she doesn't "believe in" getting sick. I don't know if it's directly correlated to that belief, but she's rarely ill. There are so many ways to think and act positively: Think healthy and you won't get sick. Expect good things and good things will come. Look for the good in someone and you'll find it. There are countless examples of how positive energy heals and helps, but there remains a lot of negativity in the world. It's up to us to change that.

A good place to start countering the negative is changing your language. Highlight the positive; talk about what is, not what isn't; outline the dos, not the don'ts. Rules go over better when you can state them positively: "Respect others by taking your phone calls outside" instead of "Do not use cell phones." Motivating an employee works better when you honestly express your belief that he or she will achieve the desired outcomes ("when" rather than "if" you get that new clien). Challenge yourself to speak about what is possible, rather than what isn't. The effects of a positive outlook and positive expression will be far-reaching. Putting positive thoughts into the world can bring them back to you.

Finally, there's a theme that I've heard over and over again when I'm coaching other coaches or managers or trainers. They tell me that those of us who want to develop and serve others are rarely being coached or supported ourselves. Who asks us powerful, thought-provoking questions? Who touches and inspires and affirms us? Too often, no one does.

Our wishes, goals, and dreams of fulfillment are as important as those of any of the people we help. Making sure our own aspirations and growth aren't pushed to the back burner isn't one of the 10 steps described in this book, but it is critically important to our success as coaches—and as employees, partners, parents, and friends.

My request for you here is simply this: Take good care of yourself. Make sure you're thinking big for yourself and loving and appreciating yourself as much as you are doing those things for your coachees.

Sure, there are all sorts of gremlin voices that tell us we don't deserve to be treated nicely, to be happy and successful and satisfied. "Why should I be happy when other people are suffering?" we might ask, or "I have it good. Who am I to complain?" (There are, of course, several other ways these gremlins make this point.) But I want to counter those voices with this point: You deserve all the goodness in the world. And whether it's directed at you, your colleagues, your family and friends, or people you don't know, the more goodness that's floating around out there, the better the world is for all of us.

In pointing out the value of taking care of oneself, I often remind my clients of this airplane safety announcement: In the event of an emergency, place your own oxygen mask on before helping your children or those around you to put on theirs. That's not an instruction for selfishness. If you don't help yourself first, you'll lose consciousness and be unable to help anyone. The analogy is clear for helpers and caregivers: If we neglect our own needs, we'll eventually suffer an equivalent loss of consciousness and be unable to help ourselves or anyone else.

You and your coachees will encounter many of these concepts (and plenty of others) as you move forward together. You're opening the door to people expressing themselves and experiencing themselves in new ways. You're going to be giving people experiments to improve their work and personal lives. You'll be spreading awareness of people's own strengths and desires. You'll be helping them become positive forces in the workplace and in society.

I'd love to hear from you what coaching concepts you're discovering. Write and tell me how you use these steps and what results you're getting. You can find my email address at my website, www.fullexperiencecoaching.com.

The world is waiting for you. Take your coaching tools and go explore your power of possibility.

RESOURCES

Adams, Marilee G. 2004. *Change Your Questions, Change Your Life: 7 Powerful Tools for Life and Work.* San Francisco, CA: Berrett-Koehler.

Bethanis, Susan J. 2004. *Leadership Chronicles of a Corporate Sage: Five Keys to Becoming a More Effective Leader.* New York: Kaplan Business.

Blanchard, Kenneth, and Spencer Johnson. 1982. *The One Minute Manager.* New York: William Morrow.

Bolles, Richard N. 2007. *What Color Is Your Parachute? 2008: A Practical Manual for Job-Hunters and Career Changers.* Berkeley, CA: Ten Speed Press.

Bolton, Robert. 1979. *People Skills: How to Assert Yourself, Listen to Others, and Resolve Conflicts.* New York: Simon & Schuster.

Buckingham, Marcus, and Donald O. Clifton. 2001. *Now, Discover Your Strengths.* New York: Free Press.

Carson, Richard D. 2008. *Taming Your Gremlin: A Surprisingly Simple Method for Getting Out of Your Own Way.* New York: Quill.

Collins, Jim. 2001. *Good to Great: Why Some Companies Make the Leap. . . and Others Don't.* New York: Collins Business.

Doyle, James S. 1999. *The Business Coach: A Game Plan for the New Work Environment.* New York: John Wiley & Sons.

Flaherty, James. 2005. *Coaching: Evoking Excellence in Others.* St. Louis, MO: Butterworth-Heinemann.

Friedman, Stewart D. 2008. *Total Leadership: Be a Better Leader, Have a Richer Life.* Boston, MA: Harvard Business Press.

Goleman, Daniel. 2000. *Working With Emotional Intelligence.* New York: Bantam.

Gratton, Lynda. 2009. *Glow: How You Can Radiate Energy, Innovation, and Success.* San Francisco, CA: Berrett-Koehler.

Greenberg, Sidney. 1998. *Say Yes to Life: A Book of Thoughts for Better Living*. Lanham, MD: Jason Aronson.

Haneberg, Lisa. 2006. *Coaching Basics*. Alexandria, VA: ASTD Press.

Katie, Byron, with Stephen Mitchell. 2002. *Loving What Is: Four Questions That Can Change Your Life*. New York: Harmony Books.

Klaus, Peggy. 2003. *Brag! The Art of Tooting Your Own Horn Without Blowing It*. New York: Warner Business Books.

Lombardo, Michael M., and Robert W. Eichinger. 1989. *Eighty-Eight Assignments for Development in Place*. Greensboro, NC: CCL Press.

———. 1999. *The Leadership Machine: Architecture to Develop Leaders for Any Future*. Minneapolis, MN: Lominger.

Lucas, Robert. 1994. *Coaching Skills: A Guide for Supervisors*. New York: McGraw-Hill.

Nelson, Bob. 1997. *1,001 Ways to Energize Employees*. New York: Workman Publishing.

———. 2005. *1,001 Ways to Reward Employees*. New York: Workman Publishing.

Porter, Shirley, Keith J. Porter, and Christine Bennett. 1998. *Me, Myself & I, Inc.: 10 Steps to Career Independence*. Manassas Park, VA: Impact Publications.

Rosenberg, Marshall B. 2003. *Nonviolent Communication: A Language of Life*. Encinitas, CA: PuddleDancer Press.

Wheatley, Margaret J. 2002. *Turning to One Another: Simple Conversations to Restore Hope to the Future*. San Francisco, CA: Berrett-Koehler.

Whitworth, Laura, Karen Kimsey-House, Henry Kimsey-House, and Phillip Sandahl. 2007. *Co-Active Coaching: New Skills for Coaching People Toward Success in Work and Life*. Mountain View, CA: Davies-Black.

I N D E X

Note: *e* represents example, *t* table, *to* tool, and *w* worksheet.

Sophie Oberstein is the founder of Full Experience Coaching, a leadership and personal coaching practice. She coaches individuals across the country who are seeking increased effectiveness and satisfaction at work, and those exploring their power to bring fulfillment and joy to their lives. She also offers in-person and teleconference-based workshops on coaching and facilitation of training.

Before becoming a coach, she served as the employee development manager for the City of Redwood City, California, responsible for the development and performance improvement of more than 650 city employees, from gardeners to librarians to accountants and police officers.

Oberstein founded and managed Targeted Training Solutions, a consulting firm that delivered engaging and effective customized training for global organizations, including AT&T, Colgate-Palmolive, Dow Jones, Johnson & Johnson, KPMG, Merck Pharmaceuticals, the Pennsylvania Horticultural Society, and SunGard Recovery Systems. Oberstein also has been a training manager for Citibank's retail bank in the New York marketplace.

Oberstein holds a master's degree in human resources management and postgraduate certification in training and development. Her certification as a professional co-active coach (CPCC) is from the Coaches Training Institute in San Rafael, California. She also is ACC certified by the International Coach Federation. She has been an instructor in the master's of business administration program at Drexel University, Philadelphia, Pennsylvania; in the training certificate program at Mercer County Community College in West Windsor, New Jersey; and in the human resources program at Menlo College in Atherton, California.

She has published numerous articles in professional journals, including "The 3-5-3 Approach to Creative Training Design" (*Infoline,* September 1996), and a strategic HR audit in the Jossey-Bass *1999 Annual.* Her first book, *Beyond Free Coffee & Donuts: Marketing Training and Development* (2003), is available from ASTD Press.

Oberstein is a past president of ASTD's Greater Philadelphia chapter.

About Berrett-Koehler Publishers

Berrett-Koehler is an independent publisher dedicated to an ambitious mission: Creating a World That Works for All.

We believe that to truly create a better world, action is needed at all levels—individual, organizational, and societal. At the individual level, our publications help people align their lives with their values and with their aspirations for a better world. At the organizational level, our publications promote progressive leadership and management practices, socially responsible approaches to business, and humane and effective organizations. At the societal level, our publications advance social and economic justice, shared prosperity, sustainability, and new solutions to national and global issues.

Visit our website

Go to www.bkconnection.com to read exclusive excerpts of new books, get special discounts, see videos of our authors, read their blogs, find out about author appearances and other BK events, browse our complete catalog, and more!

Get the *BK Communiqué*, our free eNewsletter

News about Berrett-Koehler, yes—new book announcements, special offers, author interviews. But also news by Berrett-Koehler authors, employees, and fellow travelers. Tales of the book trade. Links to our favorite websites and videos—informative, amusing, sometimes inexplicable. Trivia questions—win a free book! Letters to the editor. And much more!

See a sample issue: www.bkconnection.com/BKCommunique.

BK® Berrett–Koehler Publishers, Inc.
San Francisco. *www.bkconnection.com*